# KAREN BROWN'S

# *Swiss Country Inns & Chalets*

Written by

**CLARE BROWN** and **KAREN BROWN**

Illustrated by

Barbara Tapp

Karen Brown's Country Inn Series

**WARNER BOOKS**

TRAVEL PRESS editors: Clare Brown, CTC, Karen Brown, June Brown, CTC, Iris Sandilands

Illustrations and cover painting: Barbara Tapp
Maps: Keith Cassell

This book is written in cooperation with:
Town and Country - Hillsdale Travel
16 East Third Avenue, San Mateo, California 94401

Warner Books, Inc., 666 Fifth Avenue, New York, NY 10103
W A Warner Communications Company

Printed in the United States of America
First Warner Books Trade Paperback Printing: February 1988
10 9 8 7 6 5 4 3 2 1

LIBRARY OF CONGRESS
Library of Congress Cataloging-in-Publication Data
Brown, Karen.
    Swiss country inns and chalets / Clare Brown and Karen Brown.
        p.   cm.
    Includes index.
        ISBN 0-446-38816-5 (pbk.) (U.S.A.) / 0-446-38952-8(pbk.) (Canada)
    1. Hotels, taverns, etc. ·· Switzerland ·· Guide-books.
2.Switzerland ·· Description and travel ·· 1981- ·· Guide-books.
I. Title. II. Title: Swiss country inns & chalets.
TX910.S9B76 1988
647 .9449401 ·· dc19                                    87-26577
                                                          CIP

*In Memory of*

*MICHAEL*

*You will always be in our hearts*

# Contents

HOTEL SECTION

# *Foreword*

In this third edition of "Swiss Country Inns & Chalets" we have continued in our original goals: to present to you the most charming small hotels throughout Switzerland and to share with you itineraries that not only encompass the standard tourist destinations but also explore seldom-frequented back roads. Our guide is very personalized - very subjective. Each hotel included is one we have seen and liked. But, whether it be an elegant castle-style hotel whose gardens stretch to the edge of a deep blue lake or a cozy chalet tucked high in an enchanting alpine village, there is a common denominator - each has charm. This book is written for the traveller who likes to ferret out the most beguiling hotel for each night's stay. For those of you who fall into this category, we have done your homework for you. Months of research were spent before our travels began to find the most "promising" hotels. Many journeys led us to every little nook and cranny throughout Switzerland. Then long hours of deliberation and discussion led to our choosing what we consider only the best hotels and the most interesting sightseeing. We maintain our standard of never including a hotel we have not personally visited nor suggesting an itinerary whose route we have not travelled. This latest edition of our Swiss guide is richly enhanced by you our readers. We have deleted hotels you did not like. We have added inns you have discovered. We have travelled to mountain villages you have recommended. Your suggestions have been invaluable.

Thank you,
Karen

# Introduction

Switzerland is a country of unchallengeable beauty: lofty alpine peaks whose rugged splendor is enhanced by delicate wispy clouds, velvety green meadows tucked high on mountain ledges, dramatic rivers rushing through narrow gorges, tiny blue lakes sparkling like jewels in their mountain pockets, postcard-perfect villages where every home has flower boxes overflowing with color. For centuries Switzerland has inspired poets and artists who have advertised her glories on paper and canvas. Her reputation has also attracted tourists from all over the world. The tremendous growth in the popularity of Switzerland as a tourist destination stems from the 19th century when the ever-hearty British came, challenged by her many mountain peaks which had never been conquered. These sportsmen returned to England spreading the word of the glories of Switzerland. It all began with a young Englishman, Edward Whymper who, on July 14, 1865, at the young age of 20, came to Zermatt and conquered the summit of the Matterhorn. Whymper's enthusiasm is captured in his words of praise for the beauty of Switzerland:

*"However magnificent dreams of the imagination may be,*
*They always remain inferior to reality."*

# A LITTLE BIT ABOUT THE SWISS

The Swiss call their country Helvetia: all federal documents bear the seal of the Confederation Helvetia, CH, or Swiss Confederation. Switzerland's flag dates from the 13th century. In 1863 the International Red Cross, to honor its Swiss founder, adopted the banner with colors reversed. Swiss independence dates to the days of William Tell when the magistrates from 3 cantons, then under Hapsburg rule, met to courageously and successfully oppose the hand of the ruling landholders. It was in 1291, on a meadow near Lake Lucerne, at the Rutli, that the magistrates set the seal to the Confederation Helvetia. Those original 3 cantons, Uri, Schwyz and Unterwalden have expanded over the centuries into 25 (22 if you do not consider the semi-cantons of Appenzell, Basel and Unterwalden). Each of the 25 cantons guards its autonomy and separate identity. The canton of Berne is the capital of Switzerland and serves as the seat of the federal government. However, the Swiss have historically shunned centralization of power and so rather than have too many federal branches in one city, they cautiously maintain the supreme court at Lausanne.

Although Switzerland is a small country (barely 200 miles wide and 100 miles north to south) it has a compulsory military service, determined to protect its hard won independence, national character and peace. Every young Swiss man must enlist at the age of 20 and complete 17 weeks of basic training. Then until the age of 50 or 55 he is responsible for participating in a few weeks of annual "refresher" courses. This military force is always ready to defend the country and can be coordinated into action at a moment's notice. Often we encountered such training groups who were "stationed" at our hotel. They would practice maneuvers by day to return to the hotel in the late afternoon and often spend their leisure hours washing their Mercedes. The most humorous example of their presence, however, was at night when we would retire and find heavy combat boots lining the hall, left out to be polished. Where else but in Switzerland?

Contrary to the reputation of the Swiss of being aloof and unfriendly, we found them to be very cordial, warm, and hospitable. Not a back-slapping friendliness, but a friendliness with reserve and dignity - no less real while contained in the realm of "proper". The Swiss do not have an immediate first name, folksy hospitality...rather a genuine warmth and caring. Perhaps the Swiss dedication to hard work, their total commitment to providing excellence of service, and their respect for privacy have been misinterpreted as "coldness". Once you become their friend and they do not feel they will be invading your privacy, they are extremely charming and gracious.

## CREDIT CARDS

Many small inns, and even some large deluxe hotels, do not accept credit cards. To help you decide how much cash or travellers' checks to take with you, we have indicated in the back of the book under each hotel description which hotels do accept "plastic payment". The following abbreviations are used: AX - American Express, VS - Visa, MC - Master Charge, DC - Diner's Club, or simply - all major.

## CURRENT

You will need a transformer plus an adapter if you plan to take an American-made electrical appliance with you to Switzerland. The voltage is 220 AC current. It is best to check with the manager of the hotel before plugging anything into the outlet.

## DRIVING

*BELTS*: Seat belts are mandatory when driving within Switzerland. It is also the law that babies must ride in proper car seats.

*CAR RENTALS*: Most of the major car rental companies are represented throughout Switzerland and cars can frequently be picked up in one major city and left in another without a drop-off charge.

*DRIVER'S LICENSE*:   A valid driver's license from your own country is sufficient when driving within Switzerland.   (We recommend also carrying an international driver's license when travelling abroad.)

*DRUNK DRIVING*:   The penalties for driving while under the influence of alcohol are very severe.   Do not drink and drive.

*GASOLINE*:   The price of gasoline within Switzerland is very high so be sure to budget for this when making your plans.   If you find yourself short of cash, many of the service stations will accept payment by a major credit card.   Some of the service stations have an efficient system whereby you put coins into an appropriate slot and can pump your own gas - day or night.

*ROAD CONDITIONS:*   Highways link Switzerland's major cities and are kept in remarkably good condition.   No sooner are the snows melting in the spring sun than maintenance crews begin repairing damage done by winter weather.   Many of the smaller villages are tucked away in isolated little valleys linked to civilization by narrow little roads, but even these are well tended by the efficient Swiss and are usually in good condition.

*ROAD SIGNS*:   If you are driving, prepare yourself before leaving home by learning the international road signs so that you can obey all the rules and avoid the embarrassment of heading the wrong way down a small street or parking in a forbidden zone.   There are several basic sign shapes.   The triangular signs warn that there is danger ahead.   The circular signs indicate compulsory rules and information.   The square signs give information concerning telephones, parking, camping, etc.   Some of the more common signs follow:

# International Road Signs

 **End of all restrictions**

 **Halt sign**

 **Halt sign**

 **Customs**

 **No stopping**

 **No parking/waiting**

 **Mechanical help**

 **Filling station**

 **Telephone**

 **Camping site**

 **Caravan site**

Youth hostel

 **All vehicles prohibited**

 **No entry for all vehicles**

 **No right turn**

 **No U-turns**

 **No entry for motorcars**

 **No overtaking**

**Road works**

**Loose chippings**

**Level crossing with barrier**

**Level crossing without barrier**

 **Maximum speed limit**

 **End of speed limit**

**Traffic signals ahead**

**Pedestrians**

**Children**

**Animals**

**Wild animals**

**Other dangers**

 **Intersection with non-priority road**

**Merging traffic from left**

**Merging traffic from right**

 **Road narrows**

 **Road narrows at left**

 **Road narrows at right**

# FOOD SPECIALTIES

Switzerland is bordered by Germany, Austria, Italy and France. Culinary specialties from each of these countries have been absorbed into the Swiss kitchens where talented chefs interpret these various foods into gourmet delights.

Many guide books imply that Swiss cooking is mediocre - that it has no character or style of its own. I feel that this is totally unfair. Probably the high degree of training stressed in the Swiss hotel schools contributes to the consistently fine food and service which is found, not only in the elegant city restaurants, but also in tiny restaurants in remote hamlets. Usually every entree is cooked to order: not once in any restaurant did I see a steam table. You will find throughout your travels in Switzerland delicious fruits and vegetables from the garden, a marvelous selection of fresh fish from the rivers and lakes, outstanding veal dishes, and wicked desserts followed by an assortment of local cheeses. To complement the meal, Switzerland produces some exceptional wines that are rarely exported - a definite loss to the rest of the world. Many of these wines are made from grapes grown in the Rhone Valley and have a light, slightly fruity taste and a tinge of effervescence.

The following list of Swiss specialties is not comprehensive. It is merely a sampling of some of the delicacies I most enjoyed while in Switzerland. The fun of completing the list is left to your own culinary adventures.

*BRATWURSTE*:  I am sure the Swiss would laugh to see me include such a common fare as Bratwurste in a specialty food list.  However, there is nothing more delicious than the plump grilled veal Swiss "hot dogs" smothered in onions and accompanied by fried potatoes.  A cold beer makes this meal paradise.

*BUNDNERFLEISCH*:  In southeastern Switzerland, the Grisons area, an unusual air-dried beef cut into wafer-thin slices is served as a delicacy.

*CHEESES*:  Switzerland is famous for her cheeses.  Appenzell and Gruyere are both fabulous Swiss cheeses that I especially enjoyed.

*CHOCOLATE*:  This list would not be complete without the mention of Swiss chocolate.  Nestle, Tobler, or simply "Swiss" are synonymous with some of the world's best chocolate.   Rarely does a suitcase return to the States without a bar or two tucked into the corner.

*FONDUE*:  The Swiss specialty of fondue has gained popularity all over the world.  Melted Gruyere cheese, white wine, garlic, and kirsch are brought hot to the table in a chafing dish and the diners use long forks to dip squares of bread into the delectable mixture.

*FRITURE DE PERCHETTES*:  Nothing could be more superb than the tiny, mild fillet of fresh perch fried in butter found on most menus during the summer in the Lake Geneva area.  Be sure to try this outstanding gourmet delight.

*GESCHNETZLETS*:  Veal is very popular in Switzerland.  Perhaps the most famous and delicious method of preparation is small pieces cooked in a white wine sauce with mushrooms.  This is frequently called "Veal Zurich" on the menu.

*HERO JAM*:  This divine jam comes in many delicious fruit and berry flavors and is traditionally served with little hard rolls that break into quarters.

*LECKERLI*:   This is a spicy, cake-like, ginger flavored cookie covered with a thin sugar icing.   To be really *good*, the cookie must "snap" when broken.

*RACLETTE*:   Raclette is a fun cheese dish.   A block of Bagnes cheese is split and melted over a fire.   The softened cheese is scraped off onto your plate and eaten with potatoes and onions.

*ROSCHTI*:   These delicious fried potatoes called "Roschti" are served throughout Switzerland.   The potatoes are diced and lightly browned in butter - frequently with the addition of diced onions.


## GEOGRAPHY

Switzerland is very special because of her unique geography.   In the north-western section of Switzerland are the Jura Mountains.   Sixty percent of the southeastern part of the country is dominated by the gorgeous Alps.   In between these two mountainous areas the verdant lowlands sweep from Lake Geneva diagonally across the country to Lake Constance.

The impression one returns home with is of precipitous alpine peaks, deep mountain gorges, narrow mountain valleys, glaciers gleaming in the sun fighting the ravages of time, beautiful rushing streams, glorious blue lakes, gently flowing rivers, low timberlines, spectacular waterfalls, and soft rolling hills.   Every turn in the road offers a "postcard" vista for your scrapbook of memories.

## HOTELS - BASIS FOR SELECTION

Charm and "olde worlde" ambiance are used as the basis for the selection of inns in this guide. Some of our inns are luxuriously elegant while others are quite simple. Some are located in the center of cities while others are tucked into remote mountain villages. Our hotels vary also as to quality. Frankly, some are better than others because in a few instances we have chosen a hotel, not on its merit alone, but so that you would have a suggestion for a place to stay in a region or village we considered so spectacular that it *HAD* to have a hotel. We have indicated what each hotel has to offer and have described the setting so that you can make the choice. We feel if you know what to expect, you will not be disappointed. Therefore, we have tried always to be candid and honest in our appraisals. The charm of a simple countryside chalet will beckon some while a sophisticated luxurious city hotel will appeal to others. For some of you, price is never a factor if the hotel is outstanding. For others, budget will guide your choice. Read carefully each hotel description so that you can select the hotel that is most "you".

## HOTELS - DATES OPEN

In the back of the book, under each hotel's description, we have indicated when the hotel is open. The information given is what has been provided to us. Some of the hotels close the end of July until the middle of August. Much more commonly, many close during the spring and again in the fall. This is especially true in mountain resorts which are open for skiing in the winter then close for rejuvenation in the Spring in anticipation of the influx of summer tourists. A word of caution. We have received letters from readers, and have experienced the same saga ourselves. Even though many hotels quote a certain date to open or close, in reality, they often change the date a bit - perhaps because of weather. We have found this especially true for hotels which set June 1 to open - it is frequently the middle of June before the hotel is actually in operation.

## HOTELS - DECOR

Regardless of the category of Swiss hotel, striving to achieve a high standard of service and quality of cuisine is generally stressed over the importance of the decor in the bedrooms. The "olde worlde" charm is usually allocated to the public and dining areas, while the bedrooms are often simple and modern in their furnishings. Frequently the most appealing room in the inn is the "stubli", a cozy dining room where the local villagers congregate in the evening for a drink and conversation. Usually the stubli oozes with the charm of mellow wood paneling, rustic carved chairs, gaily printed country curtains and bountiful freshly cut flowers.

## HOTEL RATES

In the hotel section, we have quoted rates using Swiss francs. We have used the Swiss franc because the fluctuation of the dollar in relation to European currencies has created a very fickle dollar. Therefore, although it will mean you will need to do a little arithmetic, you will be able to estimate much more accurately what your holiday will cost. The prices quoted are those given to us at time of publication so expect some inflation and use our rates as "ballpark" figures.

Even though we give room prices, it is difficult to be entirely accurate because rates are so confusing and reflect such a wide span of possibilities - there are high season rates, off season rates, in between season rates. Rates also vary by the type of room: there are deluxe suites, economy singles, family units, rooms with private bath, rooms with only a washbasin, rooms with a view, rooms without a view ... the list goes on and on. Since it really would be impossible to show every category, we have simplified the selection: indicated is the range of prices for a room for two people - from the least expensive to the most expensive, including taxes, service charges and breakfast. In a few instances, two meals are included in the price and this is stated. A small number of the hotels in this guide do not have any private bathrooms - again this is mentioned.

# HOTEL RESERVATIONS

We are frequently asked if reservations are necessary when travelling in Switzerland. Booking in advance definitely ties you into a structured itinerary and if you cancel it is frequently difficult to get a refund for your deposit. Also, with a preplanned itinerary, you are not free to linger when you have fallen in love with "your" little inn. But without reservations you might not be able to get a room in some special hotel you have your heart set on. With luck you might be able to just "drop in" at some of the hotels described in this guide and secure a room, but during the tourist season many hotels fill up months in advance. Therefore, if you can preplan your holiday, we do suggest making reservations for several reasons. First, hotel space in the major cities such as Zurich, Lucerne, Geneva, and Basel is usually very scarce - even in the "off season" the cities are frequently booked solid with conventions. Second, during the tourist season the country inns are usually very busy with the Swiss themselves who love to escape to the mountains with their families for a hiking holiday. Third, many of the hotels in this guide are in remote areas and it would be terribly frustrating to arrive in some hamlet after hours of driving to find the only inn already filled. Following are several suggestions for making reservations:

*DIRECT PHONE CALL*: A call to the hotel is a very satisfactory way to make a reservation. You can immediately find out if space is available and, if not, make an alternate choice. Another bonus to calling the hotel is that you can explain your particular needs and find out what the hotel can offer you - such as a family suite, room with balcony, etc. For each hotel we have given the telephone number including the area code. Ask your operator for specific instructions from your city, but in general the system is as follows: first dial 011 (the international code), then 41 (Switzerland's country code), then the city code (dropping the zero) and then the local telephone number. (Note: The zero before the city code is only dropped if calling from the United States - it must be included when dialing within Europe.) Also, check with your local operator for the best time to call - usually if you place a direct call during off-peak hours, the price is a real bargain. Almost all hotels within Switzerland have someone who speaks English. Follow up your telephone call with a deposit if requested plus always a letter reconfirming the telephone reservation with dates of arrival and departure.

*LETTER*:   If you have ample time, a letter can be an inexpensive way to request hotel space.   Allow four weeks at the minimum for an answer to your letter.   A letter written in English is usually adequate because most Swiss hoteliers can read English even if they are not fluent in speaking it.   Europeans frequently reverse the month and date, so be sure to write the name of the month instead of using a number.   To avoid confusion, it is best to state your date of arrival and your date of departure.   Clearly tell how many persons are in your party, how many rooms you desire, and if you want a private bathroom.   Ask for the rates and how much deposit is needed to secure the reservation.

*TRAVEL AGENCY*:   A travel agent can be a great asset in "tying" together all of the threads of your holiday.   A knowledgeable agent can be of tremendous assistance too in sorting through the jungle of airline fares and routing possibilities and helping you choose what suits your needs the best.   When a travel agent writes your transportation ticket there is usually no fee since travel consultants work as agents for airlines, shipping companies and railroads.   However, most travel agents do charge a service fee when making hotel reservations because so much time is involved in correspondence, deposit checks, acceptance letters, and vouchers.   But for a busy person the assistance given and time saved when using the services of a travel consultant is often money well spent.   Choose a travel agent who is knowledgeable, easy to work with, and reputable.   Be frank about your budget and expectations.   Be candid about asking in advance as to service charges to avoid misunderstandings.

*Introduction*

*FAX:* Many of the hotels in this guide have FAX numbers which are included in the hotel information section. If you own a fax machine, or have access to one, this is a very efficient way to request accommodations. Be very specific as to your date of arrival and date of departure, type of rooms desired, number of rooms needed, and number of people in your party. Also, be sure to include your return fax number. When you fax, it is like dialing a telephone number: first dial 011 (the international code), next the country code 41, followed by the city code (dropping the zero), then the fax number.

*U.S. REPRESENTATIVE:* Some Swiss hotels have a United States representative. If so, this is certainly the easiest way to make a reservation. If you study the hotel section carefully looking for those with a representative, one phone call can frequently secure rooms for much of your itinerary. However, please be aware that the rate quoted by a hotel representative is often higher than if you were to call the hotel yourself. In addition, some hotel representatives charge a fee for making the booking. This is certainly understandable: the hotel representatives must protect themselves against the fluctuation of the Swiss franc and also cover the costs of their office overhead.

## HOTELIERS

From large hotels (where one might assume the proprietor to be insulated from the tedious day-to-day problems) to small inns, the dedication and personal involvement of the owners in the management of their hotels is astounding. No job ever seems too small or inconsequential to merit attention. It is not unusual to find the hoteliers supervising both the hotel and the restaurant. More often than not we would discover the owner in the kitchen, dusting flour off his apron before extending a welcoming handshake. The hoteliers, many having studied in Switzerland's own prestigious hotel and restaurant schools, take great pride in their profession, and management is often passed down within a family from one generation to the next.

# ITINERARIES

We have included five itineraries for Switzerland, each highlighting the entire country rather than a particular region and each designed around an individual theme. *Swiss Highlights* is written for the first-time traveller to Switzerland. It is an introduction to the major cities and popular destinations. *Mountain Adventures* explores some of Switzerland's most spectacular mountain villages and settings. *Medieval Villages* traces a journey through some of Switzerland's most enchanting walled towns and medieval villages. Saturated with history and a romantic past, this itinerary steps into an era of knights, chivalry, castles, cobbles toned streets, wenches, jousting, jesters, turrets, and bows and arrows. *Best on a Budget* was created for a friend, for anyone young at heart and travelling on a budget, and for those who seek traditional Swiss inns and yet appreciate it when the simplicity of accommodation is reflected in the price.

*Switzerland by Train, Boat and Bus* takes advantage of the country's fabulous transportation network and lets you most effectively soak in the splendors of Switzerland's valleys, mountains, rivers and lakes without having to attempt the roads and passes in your own car. Most of Switzerland's highlights are incorporated into this romantic itinerary.

These itineraries (with the exception of *Switzerland by Train, Boat and Bus*) are designed for touring Switzerland by car. There is no comparable way to travel, to explore the countryside, to really understand the depths and reaches of a valley, to fully comprehend the dimensions, magnificence and power of its lofty alpine peaks, and to experience the beauty and grace of its lakes and rivers. Cars are easy to rent and available in most mid-sized towns and driving is on the "proper" side. The roads, like everything else in Switzerland, are efficiently marked and once you get used to the excellent color-coded sign system, directions are easy to follow. Green signs depict freeways. Blue signs mark regular roads. White signs depict the smaller roads. Yellow signs mark walking paths or roads closed to vehicle traffic. Most of the roads are excellent, but some of the smaller roads in remote areas or over narrow, twisting mountain passes are not recommended for the faint of heart or hesitant drivers. It is also necessary to note that certain mountain passes close during winter months and it wise to route accordingly. However, to accommodate the winter season, Switzerland boasts some of the world's most impressive mountain passes and tunnels. While driving in Switzerland it is also wise to know that there is a road condition hot line reached by dialing 163.

## LANGUAGE

Switzerland is a country of three official languages: *GERMAN* is the dominant language and is spoken all over central and northern Switzerland; *ITALIAN* is spoken in the south; *FRENCH* is spoken in the west. The closest the Swiss come to their own language is Romanish which is spoken by a small number of people in southeastern Switzerland. English is usually spoken in the hotels and shops of tourist centers. When you are in remote areas you might need to communicate with a dictionary and a smile.

## MAPS

A map at the beginning of each itinerary outlines its route and shows suggested sightseeing and overnight stops. These maps are an artist's renderings and intended to be used as guidelines only. To supplement this book and simplify your own travels, we suggest that you purchase a detailed road map and mark your route with a highlight pen. (If you are planning to stay in some cities en route, the purchase of the cities' maps where you can pinpoint your hotel in advance is also extremely helpful.)

# RESTAURANTS

Switzerland boasts some of Europe's most outstanding restaurants. An exceptionally high degree of professionalism and excellence is maintained in even the simplest of restaurants, and the presentation and quality of food would rival any in the world. Many restaurants in Switzerland serve food piping hot from a cart - a nicety usually encountered in only the most exclusive restaurants in other countries. Then, when you have finished, not only are you presented with a comparable second portion, it is brought to you on a clean warm plate with the same skillful delivery.

Most inns have at least two restaurants. Frequently there is a central entry hall with a somewhat "formal" restaurant on one side and a "pub-like", informal restaurant on the other. The latter is called the "stubli", and if you are in the countryside this is where the farmers gather in the late afternoon for a bit of farm gossip and perhaps a card game of "jass". Locals gather after work in the stubli for relaxation, and in the evening families congregate for a glass of beer, wine, a thimbleful of kirsch schnapps, or a popular "spritzer".

# SHOPPING

Switzerland has a tempting array of products to entice even the reluctant buyer and shopping in Switzerland is fun: the stores are pretty and the merchandise is usually of excellent quality. While in Zurich do not overlook a marvelous store near the Zum Storchen Hotel that has an exceptional selection of art and handicraft items. It is called Schweizer Heimatwerk. In Switzerland the prices are usually set, so there is no bargaining and the tax is normally included in the price. If you want to pay no tax at all, there is a tax-free town, SAMNAUN, located in a remote corner of eastern Switzerland near the Austrian border. Here unbelievable prices and a fantastic assortment of items attract shoppers from all over Europe.

Following are some shopping suggestions: watches and clocks, mechanical toys, wood carvings, cow bells, Swiss army knives, chocolates, cheeses, kirsch schnapps, antiques, St Gallen lace, hand-embroidered items, fine cotton material, children's clothing, ski wear.

## SPORTS

Sports are an integral part of the lure of Switzerland. The mountains have been tempting adventurers to Switzerland since the middle of the 1800s when Edward Whymper crossed the Channel from England to be the first to reach the top of the famous Matterhorn.

The whole of Switzerland is like a gorgeous park - a paradise for the sportsman. The fame of ski areas such as Zermatt, St Moritz, Davos, Wengen, Klosters, Villars and Verbier has spread throughout the world. The glory of mountain lakes such as Lake Geneva, Lake Lucerne, and Lake Zurich are ideal for boating, fishing and swimming. The reputation of the incredible array of marked walking trails has beckoned hikers from far and near.

## SWISS NATIONAL TOURIST OFFICE

The Swiss National Tourist Office is an excellent source of information. If you have any questions not answered in this guide or need special guidance for a particular destination within Switzerland, one of their offices will be happy to assist you. Should you be planning an extensive holiday using the public transportation system, there is an invaluable book you can purchase through the Swiss National Tourist Office. This guide, "The Official Timetable", is published twice a year and contains a wealth of information. It outlines every timetable within Switzerland for boats, trains and buses. The Swiss National Tourist Offices within the United States are located at:

Swiss National Tourist Office
608 Fifth Avenue
New York, NY l0020
(212) 757-5944

Swiss National Tourist Office
250 Stockton Street
San Francisco, CA 94108
(415) 362-2260

## TRANSPORTATION

Although cars afford the flexibility to deviate on a whim and explore enticing side roads or beckoning hilltop villages, Switzerland's transportation network is so superb that one can travel conveniently by train, boat or bus throughout the country - from the largest city to the smallest hamlet. So, if you were ever thinking of a vacation without a car, Switzerland is the country you should choose. To make using public transportation easier and more economical, Switzerland offers several passes. Similar in principal to the Eurail Pass, the HOLIDAY CARD is an incredible value if you are travelling exclusively in Switzerland. It gives a choice of

*Introduction*

first or second class and enables travel for periods of four, eight, fifteen or thirty days on all trains of the Swiss Federal Railways, on nearly all private railways, lake steamers and postal buses. It also enables travel at a reduced rate on many mountain railways and cable cars. The card must be purchased outside Switzerland through travel agents, Swissair, or any Swiss National Tourist Office, and is not available to Swiss residents. Also available, but exclusively for the bus systems, are POST ROVER tickets which qualify for seven days of unlimited travel.

*TRAINS*: Switzerland has one of the most remarkable rail systems in the world, with more than 3,400 miles of track. Just over half are operated by the Swiss Federal Railway system while the others are privately owned. However, they are all integrated and connections are scheduled to synchronize both efficiently and conveniently. Their timetable is patterned after the perfection of the Swiss clock - trains depart to the scheduled second.

The train stations, often chalet-style buildings, are spotlessly clean, and many times double as a residence for the station master. The buildings are charming in their Swiss architecture. You often find evidence of domesticity - flowers cascading from the upstairs window boxes and laundry hanging on the line. The station masters are always handsome in their "toy" uniforms and most speak some English.

If you are flying into either Zurich or Geneva, there is a beautifully geared network. From either of these cities you can take a train directly to many major cities throughout Switzerland. The entire setup is wonderfully convenient for the traveller. As you exit the baggage claim area, there is a counter where you can check your luggage right through to your destination and climb aboard the train completely unencumbered. If you really want to spoil yourself, when the train arrives at your first night's stop, you can take a cab to your hotel, give the baggage claim ticket to the receptionist and ask him to send the porter to the station for your bags.

When it is time to return home, the Swiss have devised an even more impressive system for the handling of luggage. From over 100 train or postal coach stations throughout Switzerland you can check your luggage via the Geneva or Zurich airport all the way to your own home town airport. The Swiss call this "FLY LUGGAGE". All you need is a plane ticket with a confirmed reservation for any scheduled flight from Zurich or Geneva. The cost is nominal and is based per piece of luggage. If you have a railway ticket to the Zurich or Geneva airport, you pay even less.

*BUSES*: Boasting more mileage than the Swiss railway itself, the Postal Bus lines originated after World War I with the primary purpose of transporting mail. In conjunction with the entire network of railway lines, every village in Switzerland is serviced, and as buses are also available for public use, they provide Switzerland with one of the most exceptional transportation networks in the world. Depending on the demand, under the auspices of the postal bus line there are 4-to-5 person limousines, mini-buses or the ever familiar buttercup-yellow buses. In addition to the mail, the bus lines are responsible for transporting about 15 million passengers, and their dependability and excellence of service are extremely impressive.

In Switzerland, the position of postal bus driver is very prestigious. Those chosen for the job are unmatched in their skillful driving ability. Their record is faultless: in the history of the postal bus service there has not been one fatal accident. In addition to excellent driving techniques, the drivers also play an important role in the community - usually they are well versed on the local news and social activities and familiar with the most recent wedding, gossip or current business venture. Not only must the bus drivers "know every millimeter" of the road , but the training they endure is exacting and stringent. Thousands apply each year for positions available to just a few. To qualify for consideration alone is demanding and selective. An applicant must be no older than 28; have completed his military duty; and be able to speak three languages. If they then pass a rigorous physical exam they commence with years of specialized training before taking position behind the wheel. They are first assigned for several years to drive a postal truck and then a bus in the lowlands. As a finale they must negotiate a bus up a treacherous mountain road, extremely narrow with a number of hairpin turns, and then successfully complete a seemingly impossible U-turn, all to be observed and judged not by one examiner but by a bus load of veteran bus drivers. Justifiably, those who achieve position as postal driver have command of the roadways and other vehicles are expected to yield. It is not uncommon to view a bus driver assisting a petrified driver who has understandably encountered difficulty on a pass or a narrow bend and who is too frightened to move.

As the postal buses wind up the incredible mountain passes the sound of their horn, warning other vehicles of their approach, is familiar - a tune from Rossini's "William Tell Overture".

*BOATS*: Switzerland is a land of lakes and rivers and to travel the country by its waterways affords an entirely new and enchanting perspective. Often a river boat or lake steamer will depart from a dock just a few feet from a hotel, enabling you to journey from one destination to another or continue inland by connecting with either a train, bus or hired car. Concerned with preserving their heritage, the Swiss are also responsible for providing the necessary funding to refurbish a number of the beautiful and graceful lake steamers and ferries. Not only can you see Switzerland by water but also experience some nostalgia.

## WEATHER

Switzerland is a country of many climates: the high mountain weather is unlike the milder climate around Lake Geneva; the Lake Geneva area is unlike the balmy Italian lake district; the central valleys have a climate all their own. The tourist season extends almost all year in Switzerland. The only exceptions perhaps would be November when the glory of winter has not yet arrived and the colorful fall season has subsided or March when winter is losing its splendor and blossoms of spring have not yet appeared.

Winter is the season for the sports enthusiasts, with excellent downhill ski slopes, beautifully marked cross country trails, skating, and curling. Winter is also for those who simply love the charm of picture book villages wrapped in blankets of snow. Many roads are closed in the winter so your route should be carefully planned.

Summer is the most popular season. The days are usually mild and sunny and the mountain passes are open so you can explore all the isolated little villages.

Spring is my favorite time of year. Weather in late spring can be absolutely glorious - the meadows are a symphony of color with a profusion of wild flowers, the fields are brilliant green and the mountains still have their winter cap of snow.

Fall is also a good time to visit Switzerland, when the first snowstorms leave the mountains wearing new bonnets of pristine snow. The trees and vineyards are mellowing in shades of red and gold and the flowers are at their peak of bloom in every window box. There is a hint of winter in the air, except in the southern Italian lake district where the weather is usually still balmy.

A note of advice concerning the weather. As you admire the green fields, their very lushness suggests that it frequently rains in Switzerland. It is hard to predict when it will rain - weather is truly a matter of luck. So do not set your heart on all sunny days: the chances are that you will have some rain and some sun. Be prepared in heart and rain apparel, and rest assured - you will love Switzerland rain or shine.

# Sightseeing Reference
## for Itineraries

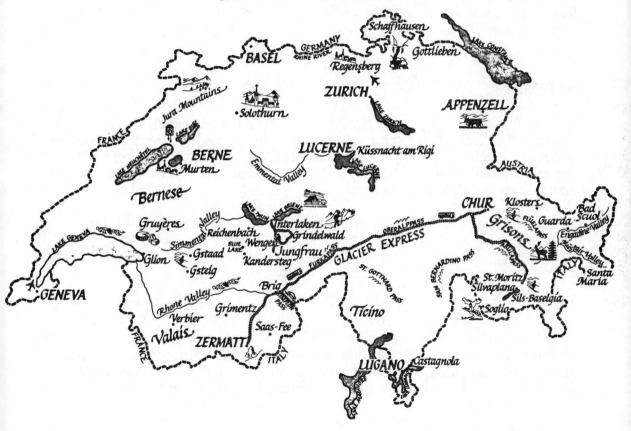

# Sightseeing Reference for Itineraries

The five suggested itineraries in this guide crisscross back and forth across Switzerland describing routes tailored for individual whims and budgets. Because certain "key" towns reappear in several itineraries we decided to have an individual sightseeing section as a quick reference of what to expect along your route. The following towns, listed alphabetically, appear in the itineraries as overnight destinations.

## APPENZELL

Appenzell is a "picture book perfect" village. The town is justifiably famous with tourists who flock to see the marvelous designs painted on the facades of the buildings, a colorful variety of artwork - landscapes, folk art, flowers, abstract designs, animals, and people. Appenzell is famous also for the local exquisite embroidery and delicious cheeses.

Politically, Appenzell is well known for its demonstration of real democracy. On the last Sunday in April, the citizens, usually wearing their colorful traditional costumes, gather in the town square to elect the representatives to their local canton. This is done with a show of hands.

The most appealing aspect of Appenzell is not the town itself, but rather the tranquil countryside which surrounds it. This area of Switzerland is magnificent, with lush, rolling, gentle green fields accented with plump, happy cows lazily munching grass to the rhythm of their cow bells. Snuggled in these lovely pastures are magnificent farmhouses: not little chalets, but huge structures where the family's home, adorned with masses of flowers, is attached to the barn where the animals are within easy access during the snows of winter.

# BASEL

The town of Basel is well worth a visit. It is an industrial city, the second largest in Switzerland. From the outskirts, the city is not very attractive, but when you arrive at the heart of the old town, you will find a delightful medieval city - a very real city functioning as a center for banking, insurance, trade and commerce. Being at the border of France and Germany and linked by the Rhine with central Europe, Basel has a very important strategic location. The Rhine acts as the gateway to the North Sea, so Basel is also a very busy port.

The splendidly preserved old town is a delight to stroll around. Here you can discover, tucked away on back streets, charming squares adorned with joyful little fountains. In the old town you will want to visit the CATHEDRAL which dates back to the 12th century. Also in your wanderings you will come across the MARKET SQUARE (Markplatz) which is host every morning to a flower and vegetable market. The TOWN HALL (Rathaus) dates from the 16th century and is beautifully decorated with Frescos. If you enjoy museums, there is an excellent MUSEUM OF FINE ARTS (Kuntsmuseum) which features works of art of the 15th and 16th centuries. Another museum is the MUSEUM OF ANTIQUE ART (Antikenmuseum) which features sculptures and art dating from the pre-Hellenic times to the Roman era.

In summer there are boat tours which offer a leisurely view of the city. This method of sightseeing is especially interesting because from the river you can view many of the marvelous old buildings which line the river and also cross under some of the bridges which so colorfully span the Rhine.

# BERN

Berne is a beautifully preserved 16th-century medieval city. It has a fascinating setting nestled on a hill which is almost completely encircled by a loop of the Aare River. Further enhancing the picture, the mountains rise in the background. The setting alone would make Berne worth a stop, but the town itself has lots of character and interesting sightseeing attractions.

The Marktgasse, the main street of the old part of Berne, has charming medieval buildings, arcaded sidewalks, intriguing shops, and whimsical fountains.

My favorite attraction in Berne is the clock tower which until the 13th century was the town's West Gate. This clock tower appeals to the child in all of us. Four minutes before the hour the "show" begins that cannot help bringing a smile: as the bell peals, there is succession of figures which parade across the clock including the most popular of all - darling little bear cubs.

Berne is an easy walking city. Just a stroll from the clock tower is the Nydegg Bridge. From here you have wonderful views of the town and, if you are a photographer, some great shots.


# CASTAGNOLA

Castagnola is a lakeside community close to Lugano. From Castagnola there is a scenic walking path connecting Castagnola with the small town of Gandria. This trail hugs the shore of Lake Lugano and makes a pleasant excursion on a nice day. To add to the enjoyment, you can stop along the way at one of the little lake front cafes for refreshment. However, Castagnola's real claim to fame in the "sightseeing department" is the VILLA FAVORITA. What luck for the tourist that in the tiny town of Castagnola is one of the finest museums in Switzerland.

The museum is located in a park like setting in a beautiful mansion on the shore of the lake and contains many masterpieces by European artists. Since this is a private museum check carefully at your hotel to find out what hours it is open.


## GENEVA

Geneva is frequently thought of as a "new" city - a city of banking and commerce; an international city housing the Place Des Nations; a city of beautiful shops; a city of museums and culture; an industrial city. All this is true, but Geneva also has one of the most attractive medieval sections in Switzerland. "Old Geneva" is located on the south side of the Rhone River. Here the hills rise steeply from the shore of the lake and the streets twist and turn in a maze of fascinating little shops, fountains, flower- filled squares, and charming buildings. This area is crowned by St Peter's Cathedral which dominates the old town. The Cathedral, constructed in the 12th century, is usually open daily. Within the church is a triangular chair supposedly the one used by Calvin, and also the tomb of the Duc De Rohn who was the leader of the French Protestants during the time of Henri IV. But perhaps the most spectacular part of St Peter's Cathedral is the climb to the top of the north tower where you have a panoramic view of Geneva and beyond to the lake and the majestic backdrop of the Alps. Also in the old town, you might want to see the town hall which dates from the 16th century. After visiting St Peter's, wander down the little twisting streets, exploring small antique shops and back alleys. You cannot get lost because it is all downhill and when you are at the bottom, you are at the lake. There is a park along the banks of the lake - notice in the park a clock made out of flowers.

On the north side of the Rhone circling around the lake is the newer section of Geneva. In this area there are lovely lake promenades punctuated with splendid flower gardens, stately hotels, small squares, and fancy shops. This too is a perfect "strolling" part of the city - especially in early spring when the tulips are beautiful.

Geneva has many museums and interesting sightseeing destinations. The PALAIS DES NATIONS is open daily except when conferences are convening and during special holidays. Usually, however, like many museums, it is closed for a few hours in the middle of the day. There are many guided tours. The palace is located in the PARK DE L'ARIANA and was the headquarters of the League of Nations. Now it is the seat of the European branch of the United Nations. The PETIT PALAIS MUSEUM is open daily except Monday mornings and holidays. This museum is in a mansion and features French painters from the end of the Impressionist period. The MUSEUM OF OLD MUSICAL INSTRUMENTS displays a wonderful collection of European musical instruments. Since you are in Switzerland, the home of the clock, you might want to visit the WATCH AND CLOCK MUSEUM with displays of timepieces from their origin to the present day.

You really cannot help being captivated by Geneva with its sophisticated beauty and international air. As you meander through the parks and promenades, you could be anywhere in the world: you see all nationalities and hear all languages. This is a city we all seem to love and share.


## GLION

Glion is a small town perched in the hills high above Montreux. Because of its superb location, with a panorama of Lake Geneva and the mountains, Glion has attracted the wealthy who have built beautiful mansions nestled among the trees. You can reach Glion by car, or, if arriving from Geneva by boat, by a tram connecting the dock at Territet with Glion. There is also a train from Montreux to Glion.

Glion's main attraction is the view. However, just a short distance away, located on Lake Geneva, is the CASTLE OF CHILLON - made famous by Lord Byron's famous poem.   This castle is well worth a visit.   It has a fantastic setting on a small rock jutting into the lake.   Walking over a bridge, you enter the Castle of Chillon where you can visit the torture chamber plus many rooms with excellent medieval furnishings.

## GOTTLIEBEN

Gottlieben is located on the Rhine just before it enters Lake Constance.   The town is of special interest because of the Krone Hotel, picturesquely situated on the banks of the river.   From Gottlieben you can take ferry boats down the Rhine to Stein am Rhein and Schaffhausen or you can travel by boat through the channels into Lake Constance.

## GRIMENTZ

Grimentz is a small, "olde worlde" farming village snuggled on a plateau at the end of the Anniviers Valley which stretches south from the Rhone Valley.   As with other Swiss towns retaining so much of their original charm, the government protects the architectural standards here.   This is a town of small Valais-style wooden houses darkened almost black with age, usually with a slate roof and suspended above the ground on stone pillars.   My guess is that the Grimentz of old could never have been prettier than it is today when each resident seems to vie with his neighbor to grow the most outstanding flowers.   The effect is sensational - brilliant blue sky, snow-capped mountains, green pastures, and antique little homes exploding in geraniums.

# GRINDELWALD

Grindelwald captures for many the romanticized image of Switzerland. It is a charming alpine village sprawled on a lovely expanse of meadows and surrounded by magnificent towering mountains. It is a popular destination for exploring the JUNGFRAU RANGE for it is as close as you can come by car to view the spectacular giants of the Jungfrau region: the EIGER rising to 13,026 ft, the WETTERHORN to 12,143 ft and the METTENBERG to 10,184 ft. From the little station in town the train departs for the dramatic Kleine Scheidegg and on to the Jungfraujoch. For further information, please refer to the JUNGFRAU sightseeing section which follows.

# GRUYERES

Gruyeres is a beautiful little medieval village hugging the crest of a miniature mountain just north of Lake Geneva and south of Berne. This is such a unique and charming little town that it is considered a national monument and its architectural purity is protected by the Swiss government. Cars are not allowed into the village but there are several parking lots strategically located on the road which winds up from the valley to the town. Another bonus for Gruyeres, as you probably guessed from the name of the town, is its location in the center of one of Switzerland's famous dairy areas...the cheeses and creams are marvelous. Stop for a famous Gruyere quiche, or if in season, fresh berries and cream - fantastic.

Gruyeres is a convenient town to use as a headquarters for a few days. The countryside in summer is exactly what one dreams about as being truly "Switzerland". The meadows are incredibly green. Contented cows with tinkling bells graze lazily in the pastures, wildflowers abound in the fields, window boxes full of bright geraniums adorn the houses, all enhanced by the painted backdrop of gorgeous mountains.

One short excursion is to the small museum-factory just at the bottom of the hill as you drive down from Gruyeres. This is a modern building which you really can't miss as it has the entire outside wall painted with a pastoral scene. In the factory you can see how cheeses are made in Switzerland in the various cantons and also watch an English-version movie explaining the process. Also, if you are a cheese enthusiast, you can make short excursions to visit some of the other little villages in the area and sample their dairy products...you might come home a little plumper, but a connoisseur of the delicious Swiss cheeses.

The secret to discovering the fairy tale enchantment of Gruyeres is to spend the night here so that the town is yours in the hushed morning and the still hours of dusk. Leave midday when the tour buses deposit their eager load of tourists and return late in the day, to sit on the terrace and have a quiet drink listening to the tinkling of cow bells, watching the meadows soften in fading sunlight.


## GSTAAD

In spite of the fact that Gstaad has an international reputation as a very chic ski resort catering to the wealthy jet-set, the town retains much of its "olde worlde", small-town, charming simplicity. In fact, in summer you might well be awakened by the wonderful medley of cowbells as the herds are driven out to pasture. The setting of Gstaad is magnificent, with rugged mountain peaks rising steeply on each side of the valley. In summer the hiking or mountain climbing is excellent. In winter Gstaad offers one of the most famous network of ski trails in Switzerland.

# GSTEIG

Just a few miles beyond Gstaad is the picturesque hamlet of Gsteig which shares the same pretty mountain valley as its fancy neighbor yet is quainter and less expensive. Being a little village, Gsteig does not offer the luxury shops nor the extensive selection of restaurants as the internationally famous Gstaad. However, for those of you who prefer an unspoilt farming village, complete with beautifully carved chalets and a marvelous little church, Gsteig might be perfect.


# GUARDA

Guarda has a spectacular location perched high on a ledge overlooking the Engadine Valley. The main recreation here is being out of doors exploring the beautiful mountain paths and soaking up the sensational beauty of the mountain peaks. However, there is some "formal" sightseeing which can be included in your plans. Nearby is TARASP CASTLE which crowns a tiny mountain in the valley below Guarda. In addition to being extremely picturesque, there are guided tours of the castle during the summer months. Also near Guarda is the tiny town of Sent whose position on a terrace overlooking the valley is similar to that of Guarda. Sent is famous for its many fascinating old buildings decorated with intricate line drawings.


# INTERLAKEN

For many years Interlaken has attracted tourists from all over the world who come to enjoy the unbeatable combination of two of the most beautiful lakes in Switzerland with some of her most glorious mountain peaks. Interlaken has a fabulous location on a spit of land connecting Lake Brienz and Lake Thun. The town has many grand Victorian-style hotels and fancy shops and restaurants. Interlaken's location makes it a prime destination for those who want to take the circle train excursion to enjoy the majestic summit of the Jungfrau.   Please refer to JUNGFRAU sightseeing.


## JUNGFRAU EXCURSION

The diagram below will demonstrate how the pieces of this travel "jig-saw" puzzle fit together and corresponds with the following text and explanation.

The Jungfrau excursion is one of the highlights of Switzerland, and one which is mentioned in four of the following itineraries. Although this is a very popular trip, unless you have travelled the route, it sounds quite complicated. It is not. But I will try to explain, step by step, how this fabulous mountain adventure is maneuvered to give you the confidence to do it on your own.

This is an expensive train excursion and since it is on private rail lines it is not included on your Eurailpass nor the Swiss Rail Pass - however, on a clear day it is worth every penny.

The Jungfrau excursion is a series of little trains synchronized to provide you with a perfect prize - the summit of the Jungfrau. The most popular starting points for this outing are from any of the following train stations: INTERLAKEN OST, LAUTERBRUNNEN, GRINDELWALD, or WENGEN.

This trip is usually accomplished as a "circle trip", providing the maximum of mountain vistas. I am going to describe the complete circle for you with the idea that you can tailor the trip to suit your special needs, beginning and ending at the town you have chosen to spend the night.

The complete circle usually begins at Interlaken Ost (Interlaken East) train station. Here you board the train for the 25-minute train ride to Lauterbrunnen. At Lauterbrunnen you change trains for the 45-minute ride up the mountain to KLEINE SCHEIDEGG (stopping en route to pick up passengers at the little town of Wengen). It is necessary to change trains again at Kleine Scheidegg for the final ascent of the Jungfrau. The last leg of your train adventure is an incredible 55 minutes in which the train creeps up the steep mountain and disappears within a 4-mile tunnel - reappearing at the Jungfraubahn, the highest rail station in Europe. It is possible to take an elevator even higher through the mountain to a vista point. From here, on a clear day, it seems you can see the whole of Switzerland. There is also an ice palace carved into the glacier, dog sled rides, shops, post offices, restaurants, etc. For this journey, be sure to take sturdy shoes for walking on the glacier, gloves, a warm sweater or jacket and sunglasses. When you leave the Jungfrau it is necessary for the first leg to retrace your journey to Kleine Scheidegg. For scenic variety, most prefer to return to Interlaken by a circle route. To do this board the train for Grindelwald where you can connect with another train which will take you directly to Interlaken.

## KANDERSTEG

Kandersteg is a hamlet nestled at the end of the Kandertal Valley. The road ends here so those who want to continue on across the mountain range for the short cut to the Rhone Valley must travel by train (if you are driving, it is at Kandersteg that you need to put your car on the train for the "piggy - back" ride through the mountain.) But Kandersteg is far more than a train depot - this is a lovely little mountain village with a stupendous backdrop of majestic mountains, a paradise for mountain lovers.

## KLOSTERS

The town of Klosters backs up to the same mountains as Davos and actually the two ski areas interconnect like a giant spider web. Although much of Klosters is newly constructed in response to the need for tourist accommodations, the town has grown with a gracious style encompassing the Swiss chalet motif. There are many lovely shops and restaurants. The town is also very well situated for hiking in the summer or skiing in the winter. The train station is the terminus for a cableway which rises high above the village to the marvelous ski runs. Also popular in winter are tobogganing, cross country skiing, curling, and ice skating. But my favorite time for Klosters is the summer when the fields are vibrant with wild flowers and the majestic mountains stand guard over this lovely little town.

# KUSSNACHT am RIGI

Sometimes there is confusion about the location of Kussnacht am Rigi because there is a town with a very similar spelling - Kussnacht - located on Lake Zurich. However, Kussnacht am Rigi is a little village on the northern tip of a small finger of Lake Lucerne. This is a charming town with some colorful medieval buildings. Since there is ferry service from Lucerne, Kussnacht is popular for a day's excursion or an overnight stay.

# LUCERNE

There is not a wealth of tourist attractions in Lucerne - the attraction is the city itself. Nor will you feel you have "discovered" Lucerne. Frankly, it is brimming with tourists. However, you will certainly understand why as you wander the charming little streets filled with colorful shops; stroll the river promenade stopping for a snack in one of the quaint cafes set out on the banks of the Reuss River; criss-cross back and forth from one side of the river to the other, savoring the romantic character of each bridge; meander along the shore of Lake Lucerne, stopping to watch the ferries loaded with merry passengers; board one of the steamers for a lazy journey around the lake. Yes, tourists have "found" Lucerne, but it is so lovely, I do not think you will mind sharing it with others.

Also in Lucerne is the MUSEUM OF TRANSPORT AND COMMUNICATIONS, one of the finest museums in Switzerland. This display follows the development of all forms of transportation and communication up to the astronauts. If travelling with children, they will be especially enthralled with this wonderful museum.

On a sunny day, there is an outing from Lucerne to the highest mountain peak in the area, MOUNT PILATUS. The most enjoyable route for this excursion is to take the lake steamer to the town of Alpnachstad and then the electric cog railway up to the top of the mountain.   From the top of the rail terminal it is only about a 10-minute walk to the peak of the mountain where there is a spectacular panorama.

Another excursion from Lucerne is to the town of EINSIEDELN to see the home of the famous "BLACK MADONNA".   The monastery of Einsiedeln was founded by Meinrad, a Benedictine monk, who built a small chapel for the Black Madonna (a statue of the Virgin Mary) which had been given to him by Zurich priests. Meinrad was later murdered by some men who mistakenly thought he had hidden treasures.   Later the Monastery of Einsiedeln was built over Meinrad's grave and a chapel erected to house the Black Madonna.   This site has become a pilgrimage, not only for Catholics, but for tourists who are attracted to the Einsiedeln Abbey, which is an excellent example of Baroque architecture.


# LUGANO

Lugano is an appealing medieval town hugging the northern shore of Lake Lugano. While in Lugano, there are several "musts".   First, you will love exploring the old city.   This is not only best done by walking, but actually must be done on foot since many of the streets are closed to cars.   Be sure to visit the cathedral of St Lawrence (San Lorenzo) which is famous for its elegant Renaissance facade and lovely fresco decoration.   Also, Lugano has one of the very finest art museums in Switzerland, VILLA FAVORITA, a villa exquisitely set in the suburbs on the lake at Castagnola.   This houses works of art from the Middle Ages to the 19th century and here you will find such treasures as paintings by Rubens, Van Dyck, Raphael, and Titian.   Try to plan time in Lugano to visit this special museum, but double-check the days and times open since it is a private museum and is frequently closed. Another "must" for Lugano is to take advantage of the steamers which ply the lake from its dock.   You can stretch your boat ride out to an all-day excursion or squeeze it into a couple of hours.   My recommendation would be to go to MORCOTE which is a charming little village rising from the shores of the lake.   If possible, allow time enough in Morcote to have lunch in the small, cheerful cafe which juts out over the water in front of the Ticino Hotel. If you feel industrious, you can climb up the steep back alleys rising from the lake front which will bring you to the CHURCH OF SANTA MARIA DEL SASSO which contains some outstanding 16th-century Frescos. Also in Morcote is a delightful private park where you will find beautiful plants romantically displayed in gardens overlooking the lake. The park is only a few minutes' walk from the TICINO HOTEL. Another fun boat trip from Lugano is to GANDRIA, another village clinging to the lakeside filled with flowers and surrounded by vineyards. Both Gandria and Morcote are photographers' dreams. Another boat trip out of Lugano would be to the small town of Castagnola. Here you can stop to visit the fabulous museum, Villa Favorita, and then, if you are feeling sporty, take a path along the lake to the ELVEZIA AL LAGO HOTEL which has a sun-drenched dining terrace overlooking the lake.


## MURTEN

Murten is a sensational walled medieval village nestled on the banks of Lake Murten - only a short distance from Berne or Neuchatel. You enter Murten through a gate in one of the medieval walls which completely surround this fairy-tale village with flower boxes everywhere and brightly painted fountains accenting tiny squares. The entire effect is one of festivity. Before exploring the town you might want first to climb the staircase to the ramparts and walk the walls for a bird's eye view of what you are going to see. Murten is like an outdoor museum. Strolling through the town you can study many of the 15th-century buildings and the walls which date from the 12th century. There is a castle at the western end of town built by Peter of Savoy in the 13th century. As you walk through the village watch for the Town Hall, the French Church, the German Church, the Berne Gate (with one of the oldest clock towers in Switzerland), and the Historical Museum which displays weapons, banners, and uniforms from the Burgundian battles.

## REGENSBERG

Regensberg is very, very special. Here, only a few miles north of Zurich, and about 20 minutes from the Zurich Airport, is a perfectly preserved medieval village "icing" the knoll of a small hill which is laced with vineyards. In Regensberg is one of the most exquisite little inns in Switzerland, the Rote Rose, which is owned by Christa Schafer, daughter of Lotte Gunthart, one of the foremost rose artists in the world. Regensberg is perfect for your arrival into Zurich or a wonderful choice for few days to relax before departing from the Zurich Airport.

## SAAS-FEE

Saas-Fee is located at the end of a little valley which branches off from the road to the famous resort of Zermatt. However, whereas Zermatt is built on the floor of the valley, Saas-Fee is situated on a small terrace high above the valley floor. There are similarities, though, between the two towns: both are closed to automobile traffic, both are excellent ski areas, both have beautifully marked walking trails, and both try to preserve the alpine chalet architecture. Zermatt is more of the "jet-set" resort with large hotels, expensive shops, gourmet restaurants, and a vibrant night life. Saas-Fee has the reputation of being more of a family resort.

## SANTA MARIA

Santa Maria is a small hamlet intersected by the road through the beautiful Mustair Valley. There are many lovely old Grisons-style buildings in the town and a very attractive church. Nearby is the Swiss National Park which is an oasis for wildlife and vegetation. The park is very popular with the Swiss who come here frequently to hike the beautifully marked trails with their families.

## SCHAFFHAUSEN

Schaffhausen is a delightful medieval city which grew up along the banks of the Rhine just above the point where the Rhine Falls, Rheinfall, interrupted the passage of the boats which plied the river. Because the boats could not continue beyond this point, the cargo had to be carried around the falls and the city of Schaffhausen grew up to accommodate the trade. There are many very colorful houses - real architectural "gems" - within Schaffhausen, many with the famous oriel windows adding colorful detail. There are also several fountains, old towers, and, of course, a castle above the city on a knoll of a hill. While in Schaffhausen you will certainly want to make the very short excursion to see the Rheinfall. Where the cascading falls reach the bottom of the river there is a dock where you can take a boat right out to the bottom of the falls. Another excursion from Schaffhausen is to the walled town of Stein am Rhein. This little town is to the east of Schaffhausen, and as the name implies, also built along the Rhine. Stein am Rhein is packed with tourists during the summer season, but it is one of the most photogenic towns in Switzerland. After entering the main gates of the little town you find yourself in a fairy tale village with each building almost totally covered with fanciful paintings. The town is very small so it will not take long to explore it, but it is certainly worth a visit.

## SILS-BASELGIA

Just a few miles south of the famous resort of St Moritz is the little town of Sils-Baselgia, located on a thread of land which connects the two tiny lakes of Silvaplana and Silser.   The Sils area is a wonderful headquarters for cross country skiing in the winter and hiking, boating, fishing, sail surfing, and swimming in the summer.

## SILVAPLANA

Silvaplana is a small town about 4 miles south of St Moritz.   There is much more of the small mountain village feeling about Silvaplana than its next door neighbor, but this is still a bustling summer and winter resort.

## SOGLIO

The mountain setting of the little town of Soglio is one of the most dramatically beautiful in all of Switzerland.   In fact Mr Isler, who manages the Swiss National Tourist Office in San Francisco, told me that a travel writer had seen pictures of Soglio and just couldn't believe they were real so went himself to confirm that this perfect village existed.   Frankly, this is how I also found Soglio: I had seen a drawing of the town in a travel guide and immediately I knew I had to see it myself. The town of Soglio is perched on a ledge high above the beautiful Bregaglia Valley. The town is tiny, with just a few little streets lined with wonderful old houses with an Italian feeling.   The church is perfect, setting off the picture book village with its high spire soaring into the sky.   The village looks across the valley to some of the most impressive mountain peaks in Switzerland.

Soglio is not only a picturesque stopover, but in addition it is a wonderful center for walking. There are beautiful paths leading out from Soglio which run along the ledge of the mountain. Chestnut trees line some of the beautiful trails and although you are high above the valley the walking is easy.


## SOLOTHURN

The town of Solothurn, one of the oldest Roman settlements in Switzerland, is a completely walled medieval city built along the shore of the River Aare. A modern industrial city has grown up around Solothurn, but once you cross through the gate, like magic you are transported back hundreds of years. This pretty medieval town has remained unspoiled. You are greeted by colorfully painted fountains, charming little squares, beautifully preserved buildings, the famous St Ursen Cathedral, wrought iron signs, and houses with brightly painted shutters.


## VERBIER

Verbier has a spectacular setting on a high mountain plateau overlooking the valley to the glorious Mont Blanc mountain range. Although the village of Verbier has the air of a newly created modern mountain town, there are still many of the older wooden chalets around to remind you that before the skiers came to this sunny mountain slope it was originally a typical Valais village.


## WENGEN

Part of the charm of Wengen is that it can be reached only by train. You can leave your car in the parking lot at the Lauterbrunnen station and take the train for the spectacular 20-minute ride up the mountain. As the train pulls up the mountain you catch glimpses through the lacy trees of the magnificent valley below enclosed by steep walls decorated with gushing waterfalls. Wengen has one of the most glorious sites in the world, on a mountain plateau overlooking the Lauterbrunnen Valley whose walls are laced with cascading waterfalls and beyond to the awe-inspiring mountains. This is a center for outdoor enthusiasts and sportsmen. From all over the world tourists come to soak up spectacular alpine beauty. Summer is my favorite time of year in Wengen when the marvelous walking paths beckon you to wander. Along these trails there are new vistas at every turn, each more beautiful than the last. If walking is too gentle for your spirit, there are climbs you can take into the Bernese Oberland. If you are going to do some serious climbing you should hire a local guide to accompany you. In addition to being a mecca for the mountain enthusiast, Wengen also is an excellent base for the excursion to the Jungfrau. PLEASE REFER TO JUNGFRAU SIGHTSEEING (page 33).


## ZERMATT

Cars are not allowed in Zermatt. However, this is no problem as there are car parks at each of the towns as you approach the town. I would suggest leaving your car at Tasch which is the last town prior to your arrival from where it is only a few minutes' train ride in to Zermatt. As you arrive at the station you will notice many horse drawn carriages awaiting your train. In winter, these become horse-drawn sleighs. In the past few years (unfortunately) little electric golf-type carts have been gradually replacing some of the horse drawn carriages.

Zermatt is not the sleepy little mountain village of yesterday. In fact, it is difficult to uncover the remnants of the "Old Zermatt" - the weathered wooden chalets weighted beneath heavy slate roofs. True, they are still there hidden on little side alleys and dotted in the mountain meadows, but as you wander around Zermatt you are bombarded with the effects of the growth of tourism: shopping arcades stretching out behind old store fronts, hotels expanding, new condominiums springing up in the meadows, tourists packing the streets. I know this sounds awful, but it isn't. Zermatt is still one of my favorite places in Switzerland for some things never change. The Matterhorn, rising in majestic splendor as a backdrop to the village, is still one of the most dramatic sights in the world. And, as you leave the center of Zermatt, within a few minutes you are again in the "Zermatt of Old" with gigantic mountain peaks piercing the sky. It is so beautiful that it is frustrating - each path is beckoning "try me". You want to go in every direction at once.

The great influx of tourists definitely has advantages too: fun little shops filled with tempting wares line the streets; cozy restaurants make each meal decision a dilemma; new hotels have opened giving the traveller a great selection of accommodations. The pride of making Zermatt worthy of its reputation has stimulated competition among the hoteliers and shopkeepers - each appears to strive to make his flower box more gorgeous than his neighbor's, resulting in a profusion of color. The popularity of Zermatt has also merited a fascinating network of trails lacing the mountains used in summer for walking and in winter for skiing. A small train runs up to the Gornergrat station which is located on a rocky ridge overlooking the town of Zermatt and beyond to the Matterhorn. There are also cable cars and chair lifts rising like a spider web around Zermatt. There is an incredible choice for the tourist - when hiking, it is possible to either choose beautifully marked trails drifting out from the village core, or take one of the chair lifts or trams or train up the mountain, from which point you can walk all or part way down. The number of tourists also justifies numerous small cafes scattered along the trails. It is truly a "gentleman's" way to hike when you can stop along the route at a little outdoor restaurant for a glass of wine. Zermatt is truly the Switzerland of our childhood books and a trip to Switzerland is never quite complete without a visit to see the Matterhorn.

# ZURICH

In Zurich there is much to see and do. On a warm day I suggest taking an excursion on one of the steamers which ply the lovely Lake Zurich. There is a schedule posted at each of the piers stating where the boats go and when they depart. During the summer there is frequent service and a wide selection to suit your mood and your time frame.

Zurich is also a great city for just meandering through the medieval section with its maze of tiny twisting streets, colorful squares, charming little shops, and tempting cafes. It is fun to walk down the promenade by the Limmat River to the lake front and cross over the Quailbrucke (bridge) to return by the opposite bank. When weary, cross back over one of the bridges which span the river to complete your circle.

For those of you who like museums, the SWISS NATIONAL MUSEUM has a display depicting Swiss civilization from prehistoric times to modern day. Zurich's FINE ARTS MUSEUM is well worth a visit. Of special interest here are some of the paintings of Ferdinand Hodler, one of the finest Swiss artists of the early 20th century. Also on display are some of the paintings of my favorite Swiss artist, Anker, whose delightful paintings capture the warmth of family and home with simplicity and humor.

For the cathedral buffs, there is the impressive GROSSMUNSTER whose construction dates back to the 11th century. This is a very impressive cathedral dominating Zurich with its two-domed towers. To add to the romance of this cathedral is the story that it was built on a site originally occupied by a church built by Charlemagne.

*Castagnola
Lake Lugano*

*Sightseeing Reference*

# Swiss Highlights

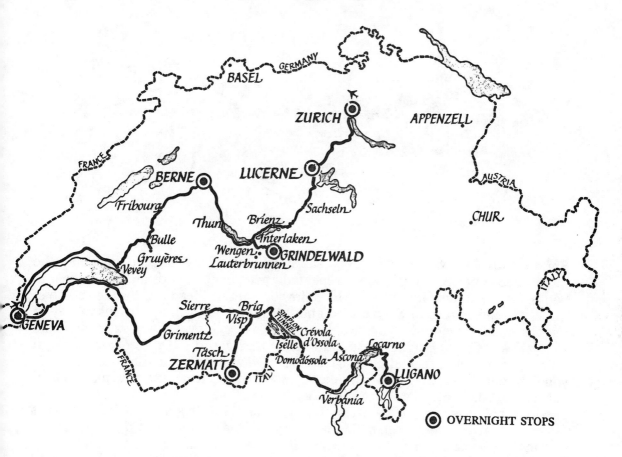

○ OVERNIGHT STOPS

# Swiss Highlights

*Zurich*

For the traveller who wants to see the highlights of Switzerland including the "picture book perfect" destinations repeatedly seen on postcards and read about in books, this is an ideal itinerary. The following path will lead you through some of the most scenic areas of Switzerland and introduce you to a wonderful variety of famous cities, charming villages, beautiful lakes, lush valleys, and splendid mountains. The towns and destinations featured deserve the accolades of loyal tourists who return year after year to savor Switzerland's stunning scenery. If you have only a few days, you can take segments of this itinerary. As an example, you could take only the Zurich to Geneva portion. If you have already, on previous holidays, enjoyed Zurich, Lucerne, and Interlaken (one of the most famous trios) you could begin this itinerary in Geneva and end it in the Swiss-Italian lake district. If your time is extremely limited, you could very easily journey from Zurich to Geneva in one day and even have time to squeeze in sightseeing along the way. This itinerary provides a framework to piece together your own custom tour of Switzerland's highlights.

If your arrival is by plane, the Zurich Airport is an excellent introduction to marvelous Swiss efficiency. As in all countries, you must identify and collect your luggage, but once that task is accomplished, the Swiss have managed to eliminate most of the hassle and have conscientiously made life as simple as possible for the traveller. There is no need to bother with porters or suffer the burden of economizing by dragging your bags along at your side, as there are usually an ample number of luggage carts neatly lined up ready for your free use. After loading your baggage on a cart, you do not have to go through any luggage inspection unless you have something to declare. Once through the baggage area, everything is well marked. If you need to make a hotel reservation, there is a desk set up for this purpose. If you want a car rental, this too is well marked. If you want to take the train into either Zurich or direct to many of the other towns in Switzerland, the train station (bahnhof) is located on the lower level. There is a train information booth just to the left as you exit customs and a counter where, for a minimal charge, you can check your baggage directly from the airport to almost any train or bus station in Switzerland. There are also many shops, a post office, banks, etc., all efficiently set up and identified. When I first came out of the customs area, pulling my luggage cart, I was concerned to notice the arrows for the train station pointing down the escalator. Again, no problem. The Swiss have thought of everything: there are directions on each luggage cart showing how to take it on the escalator with you. You can take your cart all the way to the train or, if renting a car, directly to your car.

Taking the train into ZURICH is really the quickest and most efficient means of transportation unless you have several persons in your party, in which case a cab might prove preferable.

For your first night in Switzerland I recommend one of my favorite hotels in Zurich, the ZUM STORCHEN. This is not a simple country inn, but rather a sophisticated hotel with all the amenities a large city hotel has to offer.   But do not be fooled by looks: underneath the modern improvements of the Zum Storchen there emerges the charm of one of the oldest hotels in Switzerland.   The location is excellent too - in the center of Zurich directly on the banks of the Limmat River just a few minutes' walk from where it flows into Lake Zurich.

*Hotel Zum Storchen
Zurich*

Even if you are planning your holiday as a driving vacation, I would suggest refraining from picking up your car until after you leave Lucerne. The roads are very congested between Zurich and Lucerne and there is no freeway connecting them. Once you arrive in either city there is no need for a car - in fact, a car becomes somewhat of a nuisance. Walking is one of the major attractions of both places. Therefore, in this particular itinerary, I suggest you take the train from Zurich to Lucerne. There are trains constantly plying back and forth between the two, and it is a most pleasant journey - taking just about an hour.

*Wilden Mann Hotel*
*Lucerne*

In Lucerne, the WILDEN MANN is the perfect inn within a city. Rarely do you find a hotel, except in the countryside, that retains such a cozy, intimate feeling. The owner, Mr. Furler, and his wife personally oversee every tiny aspect of this charming, antique-filled hotel located in the heart of the medieval section of Lucerne and their dedication shows in every detail.

## DESTINATION II GRINDELWALD HOTEL FIESCHERBLICK

En route for Grindelwald, head south from Lucerne toward HERGSWIL. Near STANSSTAD follow the highway signs south toward BRIENZ. About midway between Lucerne and Brienz you will pass through the town of SACHSELN located on LAKE SARNER. Take a few minutes to stop in Sachseln where you will find in the center of town a church which served as a very important pilgrimage of Swiss Catholics. Within the nave are the remains of ST NICHOLAS OF FLUE who is not only a religious, but also a patriotic hero of the Swiss. St Nicholas gained fame in the 15th Century when he is credited with keeping peace within Switzerland and furthering the growth of the confederation. A peasant, he had a reputation as a fair and peace-loving man. When there was danger that some of the cantons might go to war over disagreements, the parish priests went to consult brother Nicholas through whose wisdom a compromise was worked out and instead of having a battle, Solothurn and Fribourg joined the confederation in 1481. After leaving Sachseln, pass through the little towns of GISWIL, DAISERBUHL, and LUNGERN before going over the BRUNIG PASS. The road leads downward from the Brunig Pass to the town of BRIENZ. Brienz, beautifully situated on the lake, is a very popular resort and also one of Switzerland's centers for wood carving. The ride along the north side of LAKE BRIENZ is beautiful, with lovely views of the lake as you pass through the little towns of OBERRIED, NIEDERRIED and RINGGENBERG before arriving at INTERLAKEN.

Interlaken (the name means "between lakes") is situated on a neck of land joining Lake Brienz with LAKE THUN. The location is fabulous, with two gorgeous lakes stretching out on each side of the town plus excellent views of the JUNGFRAU. Understandably, the town has been a center of tourism for years. There are many large Victorian-style hotels, appealing shops, and inviting cafes lining the streets. Although Interlaken is a bit touristy, one can never dispute the spectacular location nor deny that Interlaken is a convenient stopover for the circle trip by rail to see the Jungfrau.

However, the suggested alternative to staying in Interlaken is to journey just a short drive beyond to where the mountains are right at your fingertips. Leaving Interlaken in the direction of LAUTERBRUNNEN, you will soon come to a split in the road. At the junction head left along a gorgeous road as you climb upwards following the signs to the little town of GRINDELWALD.

*Hotel Fiescherblick, Grindelwald*

Grindelwald is the closest mountain village to which you can drive when visiting the Jungfrau. The setting of this glacier village is spectacular, with views of three giant mountain peaks, the EIGER, the METTENBERG, and the WETTERHORN. Grindelwald serves as a perfect gateway for the train ride up to the Jungfrau and is also a haven for hikers and climbers.

Grindelwald has a number of fancy and deluxe hotels but there is a special appeal to the HOTEL FIESCHERBLICK. The accommodations are unpretentious and basic in decor but, although simple, many rooms enjoy mountain views. The personalized and homespun atmosphere is inviting and seems so appropriate in a town that is dwarfed by the magnificence of the surrounding peaks. A small hotel owned by the Brawand-Hauser family, the Fiescherblick is located across the street from the small church as you drive through the village. The hotel actually used to be the family dwelling and the artistically displayed antique farm implements are from the family farm. There is a dining room on the first floor and when the weather is suitable, tables are set out in front of the hotel.

Allow two nights for Grindelwald for you will need most of one day for the Jungfrau circuit. Allow more days if you also want to enjoy the beauty of the mountains. Grindelwald is an ideal place for either strenuous mountain climbing or leisurely walks along gentle trails.

## DESTINATION III    BERNE    BELLEVUE PALACE HOTEL

From Grindelwald return to Interlaken and then take the highway marked to THUN. If you have allocated the whole day to sightseeing, a stop at Thun, located at the west end of Lake Thun, would prove the ideal spot for lunch. Thun is a picturesque medieval village with a castle crowning the hillside. Now a museum, the castle is open to the public and from its turrets you can enjoy a beautiful panorama of Thun, the lake and mountains beyond. Getting to the castle is fun because the pathway up from the village is via a covered staircase.

Leaving Thun, stay on the expressway to BERNE. It is only a short drive and the faster road will afford more time for sightseeing. Another of the beautifully preserved medieval towns, Berne is nestled in a loop of the River Aare at a point where the river banks fall steeply to the river below. To further enhance the setting, the Alps rise in the background. The setting alone would make Berne worth a stop, but the town itself is brimming with character - truly a storybook 13th-century wonderland.

*Bellevue Palace*
*Berne*

Situated at the edge of the intriguing old sector of the city is the elegant BELLEVUE PALACE HOTEL. With such an excellent location it is an ideal base to explore Berne on foot: from the Bellevue Palace you can walk to most of the tourist attractions or wander along the arcaded sidewalks. The whole town seems to have a festive air - from its comical fountains to its jolly clock tower.

## DESTINATION IV  GENEVA  LE RICHEMOND

Leaving Berne, it is just a short drive south to the town of FRIBOURG, located on the banks of the SARINE RIVER. Fribourg is a beautifully preserved medieval city with its Town Hall, Cathedral of St Nicholas, clock tower, and the church of Notre-Dame. Although Fribourg is interesting, you will have just left Berne, which is even more colorful, so you might want to bypass Fribourg and allocate your precious sightseeing time to a complete change of pace, the charming town of GRUYERES.

Gruyeres is located only a few miles off the freeway running south from Berne. After leaving Fribourg, you soon see signs to BULLE and Gruyeres. At that point, you will need to leave the freeway. After passing through the town of Bulle you will soon spot Gruyeres crowning the top of a small hill. This village is actually one main street of beautifully preserved buildings, at the end of which is a castle, open to the public daily during summer. Gruyeres is such a wonderful little town that it is considered a national monument and its architecture is protected by the government. Cars cannot be driven into the town, but parking is provided on the road leading up the hill to the village. The town attracts so many tourists that its unique appeal during the tourist season is marred somewhat by mobs of people. However, with such beautiful views of lush green meadows and towering mountains, Gruyeres is certainly worth a detour. Another plus - this is the heart of Switzerland's dairy area: stop for a famous Gruyere quiche.

Leaving Gruyeres, return again to the highway and continue south toward VEVEY. From Vevey, take the freeway west toward GENEVA. An alternative to the freeway would be to travel the lakeside road dotted with many charming little waterfront towns. However, the traffic is very congested and the vistas are actually more magnificent from the freeway - from its vantage point, you see across the lake to the mountains beyond.

Geneva is a lovely city graced by a French influence. Geneva is frequently thought of as a "new" city: a city of banking and commerce, an international city housing the *Place des Nations,* a sophisticated city of beautiful shops, a cultural city with many museums, an industrial city. All this is true, but Geneva also has one of the most attractive old towns in Switzerland.

*Le Richemond*
*Geneva*

On the south side of the River Rhone the hills rise steeply and twist and turn in a maze of little shops, fountains, flowers, and charming buildings. This area is crowned by ST PETER'S CATHEDRAL which dominates the old town.

Geneva is also home to a string of majestic hotels which line the lake. One of our favorites of these queens is LE RICHEMOND which is an excellent choice for a deluxe hotel while staying in Geneva. Le Richemond is not immediately on the lake shore promenade, but just half a block away facing a small park.

| DESTINATION V | ZERMATT | HOTEL JULEN |
| --- | --- | --- |

Leaving Geneva, retrace your route along the north shore of LAKE GENEVA. The road has two choices: either a fast expressway or the small road which meanders through the little towns lining the lake. At the east end of Lake Geneva, take a short detour to visit the CASTLE of CHILLON, dramatically perched on its own little peninsula jutting into the lake. After visiting the castle, return to the freeway and continue following the Rhone as it winds its way down the flat Rhone Valley. The mountains rise steeply from both sides of the valley and on the lower hills are clustered the vineyards which make it so famous. The section of the Rhone Valley between Lake Geneva and the Zermatt turnoff is beautiful, but not the with the pristine beauty found so much in the other Swiss valleys since the road passes through many industrial areas. However, there are countless side valleys and intriguing passes to explore running off the Rhone Valley into the mountains both to the north and to the south. All of these side valleys (accessible by narrow twisting roads) are well worth a detour if you have the time. A favorite is a pass climbing up to the tiny village of Grimentz. The turnoff for GRIMENTZ is near the city of SIERRE. At Sierre, watch carefully for signs for the road which runs to the south of the highway.

Grimentz is a blissful little village. As with many of the Swiss towns which retain much of their original charm, the government protects the architectural standards of Grimentz. This is a town of small, wooden Valais-style homes, darkened almost black with age, usually with a slate roof weighted down against the elements by stones. It is hard to believe that the Grimentz of old could ever be as lovely as it is today, for each resident seems to vie with his neighbor for the most gorgeous displays of brilliant red geraniums. The effect is glorious with the brilliant blue sky (with a little luck), snow-capped mountains, green pastures, and darkened wooden houses with flower boxes exploding in color.

As the road is physically demanding, it is suggested that you do not undertake this side trip in the winter. But in the summer, if the day is clear, and if you do not mind a rather precarious road, Grimentz is a very worthwhile detour. Try to plan your trip so that you arrive at the lunch hour and can enjoy a local cheese fondue on the outdoor patio of the De Moiry Hotel. From here you can savor your lunch together with an incredibly lovely view of the valley below and the mountain wall facing you.

If you have taken the side trip to Grimentz, return to the freeway, and continue east in the same direction you were going before. As you near VISP, watch for the turnoff for ZERMATT. Take the well-marked road toward Zermatt. The only choice you have along the way is where the road splits and the left branch of the road leads to Saas-Fee while the right branch leads to Zermatt. You cannot drive into Zermatt as no cars are allowed within the city limits. However, this is no problem as there are car parks at each of the small towns neighboring Zermatt. TASCH is the last town before Zermatt and here you can leave your car and take the train. After only a few minutes' ride you arrive at the Zermatt train station where you will notice horse drawn carriages. In winter, these convert to horse-drawn sleighs. In the past few years, little electric golf-type carts have gradually replaced some of the horses and sleds. Most of the major hotels will send their "carriage" to meet the incoming train: each hotel has its name on the cart or carriage or the porter's cap. If for some reason you do not see "your" porter, you will find many electric taxis also available or you can call the hotel from a series of telephones next to the train station.

*Hotel Julen, Zermatt*

The HOTEL JULEN is located just beyond Zermatt's city center so you feel you are somewhat out of the bustle of the tourist rush. The hotel has a wonderful "olde worlde" charm, with a cozy fireplace in the reception hall, antiques artfully placed throughout, a charming restaurant and a cheerful little patio in the rear garden. If you are very lucky, you might even be able to have one of the bedrooms from which you can watch the various moods of the majestic Matterhorn. (Our favorite rooms are those on the top floor with a balcony overlooking the Matterhorn.)

Zermatt is truly the Switzerland of our childhood books and a trip to Switzerland is never quite complete without a visit to see the Matterhorn.

| DESTINATION VI | LUGANO | HOTEL TICINO |
| --- | --- | --- |

It is a long day's drive from Zermatt to the Swiss-Italian lake district. The journey involves travel both by car and train. In order to coordinate schedules and allow for enough time, an early departure is suggested. First you need to return by train from Zermatt to Tasch, pick up your car and drive to the town of BRIG. (This is about an hour's drive.)

If you want to include a little sightseeing prior to your journey from Brig, I would recommend stopping to visit STOCKALPERSCHLOSS which is one of the most interesting castles in Switzerland. Built in the 17th Century by a very wealthy merchant, Kaspar Jodok Stockalper Von Thurm, this castle was the largest private residence in Switzerland and is now open to the public May to October from 9am to 11am and from 2pm to 5pm. The castle is closed on Mondays. There are frequent guided tours which take about 45 minutes.

The portion of your journey by train begins at Brig. From here you travel over the mountains and across the border into Italy. You do not abandon your car but rather reserve space for it on the train as well. Try to time your arrival at about half past the hour because the train departs on the hour from Brig. When you arrive in Brig, follow the signs for the train station where you purchase the ticket which permits you to take your car on the train from Brig through the SIMPLON

TUNNEL.   After purchasing your ticket, return to your car and follow the signs to where you drive your car onto the train.   (Putting your car on the train to go over a special pass or through a tunnel is quite common in Switzerland and the sign is always the same - a train car with an automobile sitting on it.)   The signs will direct you to the road leading to the left of the station which circles over the train tracks and then veers to the right and ends up at the track on the opposite side of the station.   At this point, there are signs showing you which lane to get into for the train.   The train will arrive about 10 minutes before the hour and the sides of the train are let down level with the street so that you can drive on.   The train you require is the one going to ISELLE.   This is at the opposite end of the Simplon Tunnel and is the Italian town at which you will be directed to drive your car off the train.   Keep your ticket because when you drive off the train you turn it in as proof of payment.

Please consider, however, that if you have any problem with claustrophobia, you might not like the train ride and can, of course, always take the option of driving the twisting Simplon Pass.   But if you don't mind dark spaces, the train ride is quite a thrill: Walt Disney would have had trouble devising a more dramatic tunnel.   You enter the Simplon Tunnel (at 12 miles one of the longest in the world) and ride inside your car for 20 minutes in total darkness as the train swings gently from side to side.   The train ride is not only an adventure, it also cuts about an hour's driving time from your journey.

When you descend from the train in Iselle, you continue south a short distance first to the town of CREVOLADOSSOLA, and, only a few minutes farther on, DOMODOSSOLA.   There are signs at Crevoladossola to direct you left along a road to LOCARNO.   This is a "short cut" to the Swiss-Italian lakes, truly a spectacular drive following a river gorge.   But frankly, it is a very narrow road and a bit treacherous; so, I would recommend sticking to the main highway and heading south toward VERBANIA and then following LAKE MAGGIORE north toward Locarno.   Before reaching Locarno, you come to the little town of ASCONA nestled at the northern end of the lake.   This would be a good place to sit and have lunch or a cup of coffee at one of the many street cafes which overlook the lake. My favorite is the cafe in front of the TAMARO HOTEL. After a break for a snack and perhaps a little shopping spree in one of the ancient little streets branching out behind the lake front, continue on through Locarno and from there to BELLINZONA where you join the freeway heading south to LUGANO.

Lugano is a complicated city in which to find your way to the heart of the old section. First be sure to have a good map and next you will need patience: even though you can pinpoint on the map where you want to go, it is not easy. You might have to make several loops about the old town on the main one-way streets until you finally succeed in squeezing your way into the old section. Take heart, it is worth the effort. Although from the outskirts Lugano looks like an unattractive large metropolis, once you are in the heart of the city you discover the Lugano of old.

Tucked away in this atmospheric section of Lugano is the delightful HOTEL TICINO. Fronting a small square, the Piazza Cioccaro, the Ticino is tiny but full of charm. The Piazza Cioccaro is closed to cars, but if you are a guest at the Ticino, you can pass the barricades and drive to the entrance of the hotel to leave your luggage. When you check in, the receptionist will tell you where you can park your car. To the left of the hotel's entrance is a small grocery shop with its wares so colorfully displayed it seems more like a stage setting than a "real" store. To the right of the reception area is a small dining room - intimate and attractive. Beyond the reception desk, stairs lead to the upper floors where the bedrooms and lounges are located. A central patio is a reminder of long ago when the hotel was a convent. The guest rooms are mostly small and the decor of each varies: some are much more appealing than others, but all are clean and pleasant. On the upper levels of the hotel are various small cozy nooks, accentuated by antiques. These are perfect for reading and relaxing. Green plants and excellent original art complete the picture of a hotel done with style and taste.

Lugano is a wonderful small city in which to linger. The ambiance is more Italian than Swiss - not a surprising situation since you are almost on the Italian border. The old section of town is wonderful for browsing and the lakeside promenade a delight for lazy strolling. Most fun of all, there is a wonderful selection of boats waiting at the pier to take you to beckoning little towns snuggled along the shores of the lake. (Be sure not to miss taking the boat to Castagnola to see the fabulous VILLA FAVORITA - a gem of a little private museum.)

From Lugano, you can cross into Italy where it is an easy drive on to the international airport of Milan, or you can head north again into the Alps and complete a circle back to Zurich.

*Hotel Ticino*
*Lugano*

*Swiss Highlights*

# Mountain Adventures

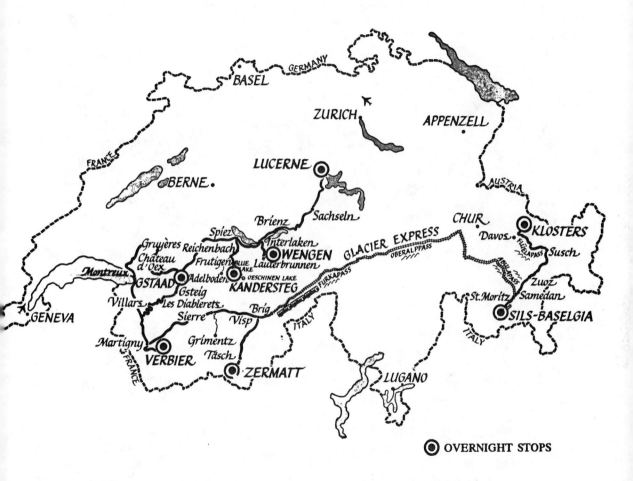

# Mountain Adventures

*Kandersteg*

This itinerary is for the true mountain lover, for the traveller whose year will be happier for the memory of a perfect sunset over a snow-capped mountain peak, whose problems will shrink into perspective as the mind wanders back to gentle meadows graced with wild flowers, whose tensions will fade as the soul recalls the stroll up a quiet mountain path.

To enjoy this itinerary, you need not be an Olympic champion, just enjoy being outside. You will be right in style as long as you have the one common denominator - love of the mountains. Of course, if you are a mountain climber, the beckoning of the Matterhorn will probably be overwhelming and I wish for you a perfect few days to obtain your desire.  If you enjoy skiing then the slopes of Gstaad will be irresistible.  However, if you simply like to meander down quiet trails dappled with sunlight and if your idea of exertion is to stoop to pick a flower, this itinerary is also perfect for you.  The mountain resorts of Switzerland teem with a varied array of Swiss and other Europeans enjoying the mountain air and the walking trails.  These holiday seekers for the most part are not your image of the disciplined, trim, serious athlete.  The majority of fellow tourists are couples or families dressed in woolen sweaters, corduroy knickers, bright knee socks, sturdy walking shoes, and primitive walking sticks laughing and talking as they meander along the trails.  Therefore, feel most comfortable, no matter what your ability, to join this jovial, friendly group of "mountaineers".

If time is limited, you can enjoy the routing from Lucerne to Zermatt and end your trip there.  Return to Lucerne or Zurich or Geneva or else head south to the Italian lakes.  However, if you can possibly extend your holiday, I would try the *Glacier Express* which is a private railroad connecting Zermatt and St Moritz.  This all-day train ride over some of the most glorious mountain passes in the world is a highlight of any trip to Switzerland.  Even if the visibility is zero, the journey on this little red train will still be fun.  What a memorable experience to arrive at the train station in Zermatt by horse and sleigh (or horse and buggy in summer), climb onto the train, settle down in the clean bright compartment, enjoy a gourmet meal in the Victorian dining car, chat and laugh with fellow passengers, and arrive relaxed and happy in St Moritz.

So, include all of these mountain villages, or, if time is short, select the resorts which sound most suited to your personality.  For Switzerland is blessed with the gift of alpine heights and lofty summits and to visit Switzerland is to enjoy her mountains.  Don't go home without strolling along some of the paths and soaking up some of the fabulous mountain vistas.

Because there are no international airports in the high mountain areas, this itinerary begins in one of Switzerland's most famous cities, LUCERNE, a charming medieval town with a fairy tale setting - directly on the lake with a beautiful mountain backdrop.  Lucerne is connected by a direct train from the Zurich airport.

*Chateau Gutsch*
*Lucerne*

The CHATEAU GUTSCH, a castle-like hotel, makes an excellent beginning to your mountain adventure. Reached by a tramway, the Chateau Gutsch is nestled on the hillside above Lucerne, enjoying a stunning vista of Lucerne and the mountain-rimmed lake beyond.

## DESTINATION I     WENGEN     REGINA HOTEL

Today's destination is the town of WENGEN in the famous JUNGFRAU area. The drive is easy and very beautiful. An early departure would be best enabling you to linger along the way. Head south from Lucerne toward HERGSWIL. Near STANSSTAD follow the highway south toward BRIENZ. On your way you will pass through the town of SACHSELN, located on Lake Sarner about midway between Lucerne and Brienz. This is a good stopping point if you want to include a coffee break with a little sightseeing. Sachseln is very famous, for in the center of town is a beautiful church where ST NICOLAS OF FLUE is buried. From Sachseln follow the highway to Brienz and then on to INTERLAKEN. At Interlaken follow the signs south toward LAUTERBRUNNEN. This is a lovely short drive but as far as you can go. At Lauterbrunnen you must park, leave your car and board a train for the last leg of your journey. As usual, the Swiss are extremely efficient and have organized a number of visual aids to simplify and outline the situation. The car park at Lauterbrunnen is well marked. Once your car is parked, follow the signs to the train station from which the trains leave frequently. The ride up from Lauterbrunnen to WENGEN is just spectacular: as the train climbs from the valley you look down as from an airplane to the LAUTERBRUNNEN VALLEY. The journey is truly magnificent, with steep cliff-like mountains rising steeply from the flat valley and mighty waterfalls cascading down the sides - very reminiscent of the Yosemite Valley. It is only about a 15-minute ride up to Wengen, but on a clear day, 15 glorious minutes.

Wengen has a spectacular site - high on a mountain meadow overlooking the Lauterbrunnen Valley and beyond to the awe-inspiring mountains. This is a center for outdoor enthusiasts and sportsmen. From all over the world tourists come to soak up the mountain beauty. In winter skiing is the main attraction. In the milder months the walking paths stretch out in every direction for the hiker, offering a new vista at each turn, each more beautiful than the last. Leisured mountain viewing or gentle strolls are matched with strenuous mountain climbs of the BERNESE OBERLAND for the more adventuresome of spirit. Mountain guides can be hired to give you advice and assistance. Remember always to consult a local guide if you are planning any serious climbing.

*Regina Hotel*
*Wengen*

The REGINA HOTEL is a prime spot to stay in this very special town. When you arrive in Wengen by train the Regina usually has an electric cart at the station. If not, either call the hotel, or else leave your luggage at the station to be retrieved later and walk the short distance to the hotel. The Regina is perched on the hillside above and to the right of the train station. Splurge and request one of the best rooms with a view balcony. Although the accommodations are bland, their very simplicity sets off the unforgettable mountain splendor. The Meyer family owns the Regina Hotel and although the hotel is large, their personal attention makes each guest feel very special - almost like a guest in a private home. Many guests return year after year to spend their holiday surrounded by fellow guests they have met in past years.

While staying at the Wengen Hotel, the prime sightseeing excursion is to visit the JUNGFRAU. This is a circle trip taken by a series of little trains to the summit of the Jungfrau where you will truly feel "King of the Mountain". Known the world over, this trip is probably the most famous mountain sightseeing adventure in Switzerland - one you will not want to miss. (See pages 33-34 in the sightseeing section for the details.)

## DESTINATION II    KANDERSTEG    ROYAL HOTEL BELLEVUE

It will be difficult to leave the Jungfrau area but when you can wrench yourself away more splendor is awaiting you. A short drive back to Interlaken brings you again to the main highway circling the south side of LAKE THUN. When you arrive at Interlaken turn left toward SPEIZ, then after about a 20-minute drive, you will see the turn-off for the KANDERSTEG VALLEY. Follow the signs towards KANDERSTEG. I highly recommend a stop about 15 minutes after leaving Spiez at the small town of REICHENBACH. There is a charming inn here called the GASTHOF BAREN with excellent food served in a beautiful country-style dining room. The owner, Jacob Murner, is the chef. Introduce yourself: Mr Murner speaks beautiful English and is a perfect host. He can assist you in making a choice for lunch or dinner. After Reichenbach you will soon come to a fork in the road: take the left branch toward Kandersteg.

At Kandersteg it will be easy to find the ROYAL HOTEL BELLEVUE as the hotel is large for such a small town. The decor of the public rooms is very traditional and although the bedrooms might lack some country ambiance, the outside "decor" is unsurpassable. Request a room with a view of the mountains. Whereas the last town of Wengen was perched on a mountain shelf, Kandersteg is at the end of a valley.

*Royal Hotel Bellevue*
*Kandersteg*

*Mountain Adventures*

A marvelous meadow stretches out from behind the hotel, extending to a majestic backdrop of mountains. There are lounge chairs on the lawn where you can sit and revel in the scenery.

From Kandersteg an endless number of walks lead off to every point of the compass, each more tempting than the last. At the end of the village a chair lift rises from the valley to LAKE OESCHINEN where rugged cliffs jut dramatically out of the clear mountain lake. The lake lies below the terminal of the chair lift and is reached via a beautiful path through the mountain meadows. On a clear day this is a lovely outing, and for those rugged sports enthusiasts the walk down can replace the chair lift ride on the return to Kandersteg. Another outing from Kandersteg is to drive to the end of the other fork of the valley to the town of ADELBODEN. To do this, it is necessary to retrace the road a short distance to the town of FRUTIGEN. At this town take the ENGSTIGENTAL VALLEY road branching off to the left. This is a beautiful drive terminating at Adelboden, a very attractive village with many old wooden farmhouses nestled on the hillside. Again, there is a fantastic backdrop of majestic mountain peaks. As you return to Kandersteg on the right hand side of the road are signs to the BLAUSEE (Blue Lake). Park your car near the main road and walk along a wooded path through a forest of twisted, mysterious trees. You begin to wonder where in the world you are going when suddenly you come upon a tiny, gorgeous lake, a photographers's dream. The incredibly blue, clear lake is set in the forest with a jagged alpine horizon. There are usually many people here as it is a favorite outing spot of the Swiss who like to come to eat lunch on the side of the lake in a little chalet-type restaurant with tables set out on the terrace on mild days. This is also a popular stop for families with children who enjoy taking one of the boat rides or just circling the lake on the twisting little path following the shoreline amongst the gnarled forest. The effect is rather like a scene from *Hansel and Gretel*.

Kandersteg is also well known as the point at which the road ends and only the train continues on to the Rhone Valley. For those travelling by car in this direction the car can be put "piggyback" on the train for the ride through the mountains to BRIG.

It is not a long journey from Kandersteg to GSTAAD.   Retrace the half-hour drive back toward Spiez, and almost as soon as you reach the main road running along the shore of Lake Thun there is a branch off to the left which follows the lovely SIMMENTAL VALLEY.   In less than an hour you should reach the turnoff to Gstaad and then it is only another two miles to the town where, located on a corner of the main street about midway though town, is the POSTHOTEL ROSSLI, a convenient hotel choice.

*Posthotel Rossli*
*Gstaad*

The Posthotel Rossli is another example of the professionally managed, small, chalet-type hotels which has passed down from father to son. There are two excellent restaurants, one on each side of the main entrance hall, both done with a charming country motif. The present owner-manager, Ruedi Widner, is also a celebrated local mountaineer and has a reputation as an excellent winter ski guide.

In spite of the fact that it has an international reputation as a very chic ski resort catering to the wealthy jet set, Gstaad retains much of its "olde worlde", small town, charming simplicity. In fact, in summer you might awaken to the melody of cow bells as the herds are driven out to pasture. The setting of Gstaad is magnificent with the surrounding rugged mountain peaks. In summer the hiking or mountain climbing is excellent and in winter Gstaad offers one of the most famous network of trails for skiing in Switzerland.

## DESTINATION IV        VERBIER       HOTEL ROSALP

One of the most scenic routes to Verbier is to continue on the road beyond Gstaad through the small village of GSTEIG. Gsteig is situated at the end of the valley and from this point the road climbs sharply and twists and turns up the mountain via LES DIABLERETS and the famous ski resort of VILLARS and on down to the main highway of the RHONE VALLEY. This is a beautiful drive but probably closed in winter and in summer only recommended for those who enjoy mountain driving.

For the more faint of heart the easier driving route would be to return to the main highway and turn left toward CHATEAU D'OEX and on to GRUYERES. On this alternate routing the HOSTELLERIE ST GEORGES in Gruyeres would serve as an excellent stop for lunch. Sample some of the Gruyere cheese served in the famous Swiss quiche and if berries are in season they are a "must".

*Hotel Rosalp*
*Verbier*

Just a few miles beyond Gruyeres the road joins the main freeway.   At this point turn south toward MONTREUX.  On the approach to LAKE GENEVA, the highway splits and you will need to go south through the Rhone Valley to the town of MARTIGNY.  Here turn right off the highway and follow the signs toward VERBIER.  The road winds through a small valley until suddenly just before Verbier it begins a series of hairpin turns and climbs sharply up the mountainside.

76                                *Mountain Adventures*

Upon arrival in the famous mountain village of Verbier, secure reservations at the HOTEL ROSALP whose most outstanding claim to fame is Roland Pierroz, the owner, who is also the chef. Even other hoteliers (themselves gourmet chefs) proclaim Mr Pierroz to be one of the finest chefs in the country. Situated on the side of the mountain with glorious views of the Mont Blanc range, the Hotel Rosalp makes a perfect choice in which to enjoy the resort village of Verbier and feast on the skiing, hiking and food. Although the village of Verbier has the air of a newly created modern mountain town, there are still many of the older wooden chalets around to remind you that before the skiers came to this mountain slope it was originally a typical Valais village.

## DESTINATION V  ZERMATT  SEILER HOTEL MONTE ROSA

From Verbier head back down the winding mountain road to Martigny and join the main highway travelling through the Rhone Valley. Follow the Rhone River Valley, noting the many famous vineyards clinging to the steep mountainsides. Unfortunately the scenery suffers a bit from the inevitable commercialization of the area, but if the day is clear and you are not in a rush, there are a number of little valleys branching off into box-like canyons to explore.

One of the most attractive side excursions would be to brave the exciting, but somewhat spine-tingling, mountain road transecting the VAL D'ANNIVIERS and leading up to the town of GRIMENTZ. The turnoff is near the town of SIERRE. As you take the road up the valley, follow the left fork of the road when it splits and continue on to Grimentz, a beautifully preserved Valais village high up on a mountain ridge. In summer it is a pretty sight with the dark weathered wooden Valais buildings set off in glorious splendor by window boxes filled with brilliant red geraniums. Enjoy fondue and the valley views from the deck of the Hotel du Moiry before retracing your steps this time down the road.

As you approach VISP there will be signs directing you to the famous mountain retreat of ZERMATT. As cars are not allowed in the town, it is necessary to park your car in TASCH and board the train for the remainder of your journey. Zermatt sits at the base of the Matterhorn, and almost as legendary as the familiar peak itself are the Seiler family hotels. It was from his doorstep on July 13,1865 that Alexander Seiler, owner of the MONTE ROSA, bad farewell to the historic group of seven who were the first to conquer the Matterhorn. Leading the expedition was Edward Whymper who returned to England filled with enthusiasm for Switzerland and for the Monte Rosa. When asked where to stay in Zermatt he always replied, "Go to the Monte Rosa - to Seiler's".

*Seiler Hotel Monte Rosa*
*Zermatt*

Be sure to spend several days in Zermatt. If you enjoy walking, there are endless possibilities. Not only do trails spider-web out of the village in every direction, but trams and cable cars climb the mountains, tempting one to wander through the glorious high mountain meadows.

When it is time to depart Zermatt, there are two possibilities for transportation: car or train. We highly recommend taking the Glacier Express, a privately owned train which departs Zermatt in the morning heading north to Brig, then continuing east, threading through the end of the Rhone Valley, passing through the FURKA PASS TUNNEL, climbing over the OBERALPPASS and the ALBULAPASS, before dropping down into ST MORITZ. This jolly bright-red train is the perfect way to traverse this spectacular, awe-inspiring route.

Reservations must be made in advance for the Glacier Express. At the same time you reserve your seat, make your luncheon reservation or else you probably will not be able to enjoy the fun of dining in the quaint, wooden-paneled, Victorian dining car. Reservations for the Glacier Express can be made through: FRENCH NATIONAL RAILROADS, 610 Fifth Avenue, New York, NY 10020, Telephone (212) 582-2110.

If you do choose to take the train, it will take a little preplanning. Although the Glacier Express begins its journey in Zermatt, you can't get rid of your car in Zermatt since no cars are allowed into the village. Therefore, you will need to drop off your car in Brig and pick up the train there. Be sure to choose a car rental company which has an agency in Brig and will allow you to turn in your car - Hertz is one that does. Allow enough time to drive to Brig, find the Hertz outlet, complete the paperwork and not miss the train - it will leave right on schedule.

To avoid the hassle of carrying luggage, upon arrival in Brig stop first at the station to leave your bags and then turn in your rental car. The Hertz office is located a few blocks behind the train station. At the time of writing, the train departs Brig at 10:25am, arriving in St Moritz at 4:48pm. Since schedules do change, please reconfirm the departure time.

Note: Another possibility would be to drop your rental car off in Brig before going into Zermatt (there are frequent trains linking the two towns). This option actually makes a lot of sense since you will save a few days' car rental cost and be able to board the Glacier Express in Zermatt.

It will be late afternoon when you arrive in St Moritz. Pick up your rental car (don't forget to reserve one) and then drive south for about 20 minutes to SILS-BASELGIA. This stopover was chosen instead of St Moritz because the town, in my estimation, has more charm. St Moritz is very famous and beautifully situated, but there is so much new and modern construction that the cozy, small Swiss town ambiance is gone. Instead, drive the short distance to Sils and stay at the sophisticated but charming HOTEL MARGNA. The hotel is near the very quaint little towns of Sils-Maria and Sils-Baselgia (you can walk to both from the hotel). The hotel is built on a narrow and densely wooded thread of land running between the Silser-See and the Silverplaner-See. Both of these small picturesque lakes are beautiful and add a gorgeous foreground to the overshadowing, magnificent mountains which surround the entire valley.

Once a patrician home of a "homesick" Engadineer, Johann Josty, the beautiful Hotel Margna is not a simple rustic inn, but rather benefits from the amenities that a large, deluxe hotel can offer without losing the feeling of intimacy. Antiques abound, accented by colorful bouquets of flowers.

As in each of the mountain retreats in this itinerary, the Sils area is a perfect headquarters for hiking in summer and skiing in winter. Because the two lakes are so close to the hotel, the summer also offers boat rides on the lake, wind surfing and fishing, etc. All in all a delightful stopover. Should your arrival be in winter, St Moritz is nearby, but even more popular is the cross country skiing available just steps from the hotel.

*Hotel Margna*
*Sils-Baselgia*

Only about an hour and a half from Sils is KLOSTERS, reached by a scenic drive that follows the INN RIVER VALLEY north through St Moritz, SAMEDAN and ZUOZ.   Zuoz has a colorful main square with a fountain in the middle and is a nice place to break your journey.   The fountain is a bear standing on its hind legs and was the emblem of the Plantas family, prominent in the history of this region. Also in the town are many beautifully preserved Engadine style buildings of heavily plastered walls painted in various colors decorated with flowers, shields or geometric designs.

After Zuoz, just before SUSCH, turn left and go over the FLUELAPASS.   As you drop down to the next valley, in the distance is the city of DAVOS.   A famous ski resort, Davos originally developed as a health spa and is now a maze of high rise buildings to accommodate the winter crowds.   On its outskirts is a lovely lake - the DAVOSER SEE.   In summer the promenade around the lake is obviously a favorite of many strollers.

Just beyond Davos the road drops down into the LANQUART VALLEY where the village of Klosters is encompassed by the rugged SILVRETTA MOUNTAIN PEAKS.   They are magnificent in their splendor, contrasting dramatically with the valley which is soft and gentle.   In the fall new-mown meadows, velvet green in color, await the return of cattle from their alpine pastures.   The setting is very peaceful and extremely scenic.

The town of Klosters backs up to the same mountains as Davos and actually the two ski areas interconnect like a giant spider web.   Although Klosters is also a new town in the sense that most of the construction has been completed in recent years, the town has grown with a gracious style embracing the Swiss chalet motif into its many lovely shops and restaurants.   The town is very well situated for hiking in the summer or skiing in the winter. The train station is also the terminus for a cable way up the mountain. Klosters is famous too as a center for ice skating and tobogganing. However it is in summer that Klosters is most regal in her beauty. There are many hotels in Klosters but my favorite is the CHESA GRISCHUNA, a small chalet-style hotel only about a block from the railroad station.

*Chesa Grischuna, Klosters*

The Chesa Grischuna is a family operation, attentively and lovingly owned and managed by the Guler family. The Chesa Grischuna oozes with "olde worlde" charm combining antiques, old beams, copper and flowers with great taste. The decor in the dining rooms is very romantic and the food, graciously and professionally served, is outstanding.

From Klosters it is only about a half hour's drive until you meet the freeway to continue on to Zurich or Lucerne.

# Medieval Villages

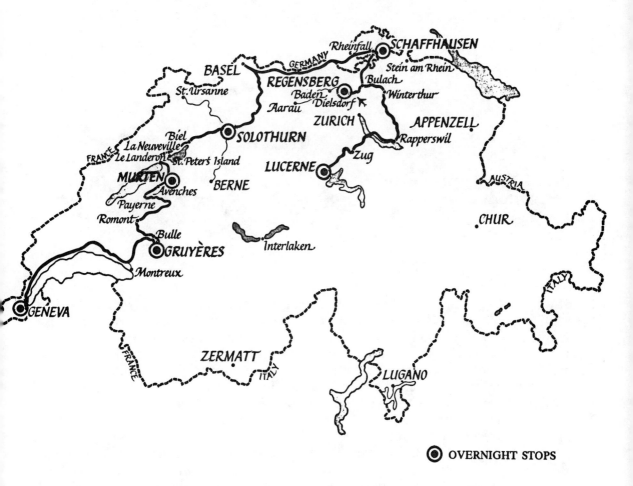

Rheinfall  SCHAFFHAUSEN
GERMANY  Stein am Rhein
BASEL  REGENSBERG  Bulach
St. Ursanne  Baden  Winterthur
Aarau  Dielsdorf
ZURICH  APPENZELL
Biel  SOLOTHURN  Rapperswil
La Neuveville  Zug
FRANCE  Le Landeron  St. Peter's Island  LUCERNE
MURTEN  AUSTRIA
Avenches  BERNE
Payerne  CHUR
Romont
Bulle  Interlaken
GRUYÈRES  ITALY
Montreux
GENEVA
ZERMATT
FRANCE  ITALY  LUGANO

⊙ OVERNIGHT STOPS

# Medieval Villages

*Murten*

Switzerland has some of the most enchanting and remarkably well preserved medieval villages in Europe. Scattered across her countryside are towns whose character and atmosphere allude to a style of life that slipped by many centuries ago. Walled ramparts often enclose a maze of twisting, narrow streets, stone buildings, painted fountains, intricate clock towers, turrets and a wealth of history. Sometimes capping the crest of a hill or perched precariously on a valley's ledge, these villages captivate the imagination and are fascinating to explore.

This itinerary wanders from Lucerne to Geneva through glorious countryside and intriguing medieval towns. If you are the "second time around" traveller who has already followed the standard tourist trail between Zurich and Geneva via Lucerne and Interlaken and who would like to discover Switzerland with a different approach and emphasis, this itinerary might be perfect for you. Another possibility for this routing would be to use it in conjunction with the "Swiss Highlights" itinerary - the two dovetail perfectly to complete a circle of Switzerland. The true medieval village connoisseur among you will say that many of the walled villages have been left out. This is true. There are many others scattered throughout Switzerland, but these are some of my favorites and are spaced in such a way as to map a delightful journey.

## ORIGINATING CITY     LUCERNE     WILDEN MANN HOTEL

LUCERNE, with its magical setting, is a delightful starting point for this itinerary since it serves as a wonderful introduction to Switzerland and offers a tempting sampling of what is to come - lakes, mountains, a twisting river, wonderful bridges, colorful flowers, fountains, boats, decorative buildings, and beautifully preserved old towns.

Remnants of stone walls serve to trace an outline around the old town of Lucerne. Although the ramparts which once encircled the city have deteriorated with time, the old section remains a marvelously preserved example of a medieval city, an exceptionally attractive one: a river winds through the town as it meanders down to the lake; stately old buildings line the river which is frequently enhanced by architecturally lovely old bridges spanning the water. Built in the 14th Century, the KAPELLBRUCKE is one of the most famous of these bridges. With its wooden roof, walls painted with murals, and even a little chapel midway, this delightful bridge has almost become a trademark of Lucerne.

To complement the theme of this itinerary, the WILDEN MANN is both a logical and delightful choice for a hotel. It is located right in the center of the old town and dates back to the beginning of the 16th Century. There is a fascinating series of scenes in the dining room of the Wilden Mann: encased in frames of glass are a set of scenes depicting the Wilden Mann from its early days until now. Look carefully and you will see in the first scene an actual drawbridge in front of the hotel. As the centuries progressed the moat was covered over and replaced by a street.

Once happily ensconced in the Wilden Mann, you will find the whole of Lucerne within walking distance - just waiting to be explored.

## DESTINATION I          REGENSBERG          ROTE ROSE

From Lucerne head north towards ZURICH. You might want to deviate from the highway about 20 minutes after leaving Lucerne to stop at the town of ZUG located at the north end of the ZUGER-SEE (Lake Zug). Zug is a very old city with many buildings dating back to the 15th Century with a small core within the old city which is still a perfectly walled enclave entered through a gateway under the clock tower. Soon after leaving Zug change directions and follow a road heading south along the ZURICH SEE and watch for signs to RAPPERSWIL located on a small peninsula that juts out into Lake Zurich. Rapperswil has a wonderful location on the banks of the lake, many colorful squares and exceptionally preserved medieval buildings. A majestic castle, on a rise in the middle of town, contains the POLISH MUSEUM. During World War II many of the art treasures of Poland were smuggled out of the country and brought here for safe keeping. Many still remain and are on display at the museum.

From Rapperswil continue north for approximately 30 minutes to WINTERTHUR. This is quite a large commercial city, but the central section still retains a great deal of medieval charm. The most interesting section is near the train station. Nearby, one of the main streets has been closed to all but pedestrian traffic and has a variety of shops housed in quaint medieval buildings. Only a short walk farther on is one of the most famous museums in Switzerland, the GALERIE OSKAR REINHART, truly an exquisite small museum. It houses works by the famous European artists from the 18th to the 20th Centuries beautifully displayed in lovely natural lighting. Especially enjoyable are the paintings by Anker who captured the warmth and charm of family life in Switzerland in the same way that Carl Larsen did in Sweden. The museum is usually closed on Monday mornings and every day from noon to 2pm.

From Winterthur head west toward BULACH - about a 20-minute drive. Upon arrival in Bulach follow carefully the signs heading west towards DIELSDORF - another 10 minutes beyond Bulach. The town of REGENSBERG is just on the western outskirts of Dielsdorf, perched on a nearby hilltop.

Regensberg is very, very special. Within only a few miles of Zurich is this perfectly preserved medieval village "icing" the knoll of a small hill. Vineyards climb up to the little town whose atmosphere beckons you back 500 years. Lodged in this romantic village is one of the most exquisite little inns in Switzerland, the ROTE ROSE, owned by Christa Schafer who is without doubt one of the most charming hoteliers in the world.

As the Rote Rose has only five accommodations, reservations are strongly recommended. A couple of days could easily be devoted to this area. A day would be well spent exploring the tiny town of Regensberg itself, enjoying the comfort of the Rote Rose, wandering through the romantic rose garden, and sampling the menu of the adjacent gourmet restaurant, the Krone. Christa's mother, Lotte Gunthart, is one of the world's foremost painter of roses and there is a small art gallery and gift shop in the inn which is open every afternoon (except Sundays and holidays) from 2pm to 6pm. It is possible to spend several hours here if you want to purchase some rose prints as the selection is quite large. Also available at the shop are many books on roses, and other gift items.

*Rote Rose, Regensberg*

An excursion to circle some of the walled villages in the Regensberg area might also prove of interest. It is only about a 20-minute drive to the ancient spa town of BADEN. As you approach Baden it looks like a rather industrial town, but be

*Medieval Villages*

patient and head for the core of the old village. Here you will discover, hovering above the banks of the Limmat River, the charm of yesteryear. Baden has many wonderful old gaily-painted houses with steep roofs and dormer windows which step down the hillside in columns until the last row becomes the river bank itself. A covered wooden bridge sets a picturesque scene at the middle of the old section of town and a church with a high steeple sets the backdrop to the picture. This spa town of Baden has been famous since Roman times and its water especially popular for the treatment of arthritis.

From Baden drive on to AARAU, another beautifully preserved medieval town. Like Baden, as you approach the town it looks like an industrial city, as indeed it is - being famous for textiles. However, the center of the old town is delightful, with narrow twisting streets, colorful houses with steep brown roofs, frequently with fresco decorations under the eaves, and carved little bay windows jutting out over the tiny streets. Aarau is a perfect town for strolling.

I am sure Christa Schafer, your hostess at the Rote Rose, can add her favorites of other excursions to take from Regensberg if you can tear yourself away from your own snug little apartment - your own little castle on a hill.


## DESTINATION II   SCHAFFHAUSEN   RHEINHOTEL FISCHERZUNFT

As the drive is very short, you can make a leisurely departure from Regensberg and still arrive in time for lunch in SCHAFFHAUSEN. Here you will easily find your hotel, the RHEINHOTEL FISCHERZUNFT, aptly named because it has a superb location right on the pedestrian promenade running along the Rhine. There is interesting sightseeing in the Schaffhausen area and the Rheinhotel Fischerzunft, managed by the owners Andre and Doreen Jaeger-Soong, is a delightful place to stay. If you really want to splurge, request a suite overlooking the Rhine.

*Rheinhotel Fischerzunft*
*Schaffhausen*

The town of Schaffhausen is a well preserved, walled, medieval city. It developed as a result of the Rhine traffic and resultant commerce. To the west of town is the RHEINFALL (waterfall) whose cascading waters halted the flow of river traffic. Arrangements had to be made to circumvent the falls and transport the cargo by land.  As a result, Schaffhausen grew to accommodate the tradesmen with housing and food.  In town are a number of painted houses with quaint projecting windows called "oriel" windows.  There are also several delightful fountains, old towers, and, of course, a castle on a knoll above the city.

While in Schaffhausen you will certainly want to make the very short excursion to see the Rheinfall.  Where the water comes leaping down, there is a park and a concession where you can take a boat right out to the bottom of the falls.

Another excursion from Schaffhausen is a visit to the walled town of STEIN AM RHEIN.  Although packed with tourists during the summer season, it nevertheless looks like a fairy tale village, with each building almost completely covered in colorful paintings and designs.  An option would be to take the ferry from Schaffhausen to Stein am Rhein for lunch and make it a day's outing.  Ferry schedules are available at the Rheinhotel Fischerzunft and also at the ticket booth on the dock, just steps from your hotel.

## DESTINATION III          SOLOTHURN          HOTEL KRONE

To reach SOLOTHURN, head south following the signs for Zurich, but before entering the city, turn east following the signs to BASEL, a convenient stop on the way to Solothurn.  Basel, in spite of its size, still retains a wonderful ambiance of "olde worlde" charm.  As you approach, the old section of town is easy to find - identified by the two towering spires of the cathedral.  From the Munster Platz you can explore most of the old section on foot.

From Basel it is a short and easy drive to Solothurn.  Solothurn might appear unattractive on the outskirts, but once you pass through the medieval wall the modern world is left behind and you enter a sector of the town that transports you back through the centuries.  You should not have a problem finding the HOTEL KRONE.  It is on one of the main streets and faces the plaza in front of the large cathedral of ST URSEN.  The bedrooms in the main building are large and airy, while the rooms in the newer section are very small.  Splurge and ask for one of the more spacious rooms - the difference is worth it.  The main dining room at the Krone is charming and always busy with not only tourists but also the local citizens. The Krone seems to be the center for much of the social life in town with wedding receptions, business meetings, and parties.

*Hotel Krone, Solothurn*

*Medieval Villages*

The town of Solothurn is one of the oldest Roman settlements in the Alps. With many squares, fountains, and colorful buildings it is a fun town for meandering. It will not take you long to see the whole city so I would suggest some other sightseeing excursions from Solothurn. One day drive up into the JURA MOUNTAINS to visit the little walled town of ST URSANNE which you enter by crossing the river and passing through the quaint gates. St-Ursanne is located in a beautiful section of Switzerland famous for the breeding of colts. In the summer there are rolling green meadows with splendid-looking horses grazing and adorable colts frolicking in the fields.

Another excursion from Solothurn is a visit to BERNE, a wonderful old city brimming with whimsical fountains, colorful squares, arcaded shops, and perfectly preserved medieval buildings. Another side trip is the 35-minute ferry ride to the stork colony of ALTREU.

## DESTINATION IV     MURTEN     VIEUX MANOIR AU LAC

Although it is just a short drive from Solothurn to MURTEN, there are a couple of walled villages along the way. Leaving Solothurn, take the highway west toward BIEL. Biel is another picturesque medieval town, but if time is short it might be best to bypass Biel and continue directly on to the tiny town of LA NEUVEVILLE, a pretty walled village on the banks of Biel Lake. Near La Neuveville is ST PETER'S ISLAND where Jean-Jacques Rousseau stayed in 1765. By taking a boat from La Neuveville, it is possible to visit the island and see the house where Rousseau lived. Farther along the shore from Neuveville is another outstanding miniature walled village, LE LANDERON. In summer both Le Landeron and La Neuveville are sensational, with masses of flowers, picturesque buildings, brightly painted fountains, clock towers, little shops, and outside cafes. But, do not linger too long - your next destination is even more inviting. Murten, snuggled along the banks of Lake Murten, is a fairy tale village. The best vantage point for viewing the town is from the top of the ramparts that surround it. The town deserves to be lazily wandered to fully enjoy the twisting little streets, fountains, old buildings, and little squares.

*Vieux Manoir au Lac*
*Murten*

Settle tonight at LE VIEUX MANOIR AU LAC, located on the lake shore only about a half mile to the south of Murten. An old manor house set in its own beautiful gardens, the hotel is a relaxing spot to stay, perhaps to take some countryside walks. The food is absolutely delicious and impeccably served. The bedrooms vary in size and decor but they are all nice. Try for a room overlooking the lake.

*Medieval Villages*

Your next destination, the picturesque town of GRUYERES, is just a short drive along the main highway from Murten.   To extend your journey and include some sightseeing into your day, I would suggest the following detours.   First, instead of returning to the main highway, drive south along LAKE MURTEN.   Soon after you pass the south end of the lake you come to the town of AVENCHES.   It is hard to believe as you look at this sleepy little hamlet of about 2,000 that in the 1st and 2nd centuries it was a powerful Roman city boasting a population of over 20,000.   You can grasp the mood of this "lost city" of the Romans when you visit the amphitheater built to seat 10,000.   In a tower over the amphitheaters entrance is a museum displaying some of the artifacts found in the excavations and an interesting pottery collection.

Another excursion en route to Gruyeres would be to travel just south of Avenches to the town of PAYERNE and visit its famous 11th-century abbey.   This Benedictine Abbey is supposed to have been founded by the Empress Adelheid, wife of the Emperor Otto I.   The church is one of the finest examples of Romanesque architecture in Switzerland with simple lines but marvelous proportions and use of golden limestone and grey sandstone.

ROMONT, a small walled, medieval town, is also on the way to Gruyeres.   To reach Romont it is necessary to travel the small country roads leading southeast from Payerne - about a half hour's drive.   The town was built by Peter II of Savoy in the 13th century and has a very picturesque site on the knoll of a hill overlooking the Glane Valley.   From Romont continue southeast on the small road toward BULLE.   Just beyond Bulle the small town of Gruyeres will appear ahead of you crowning the top of a miniature mountain.   To reach Gruyeres you wind up the little road toward the village, but you cannot take your car into the town itself as it is closed to traffic.   However, there are several car parks near the town.   The

HOSTELLERIE DES CHEVALIERS is located just above the car park at the entrance to the town. As you look at the hotel from the parking area, the hotel appears pleasant but nothing special. However, looks are deceiving because although the entrance to the hotel is not outstanding, the rooms in the rear of the hotel open out to a lovely mountain vista. The dining rooms of the hotel are in an entirely separate building to the right of the hotel section and, although the bedrooms are simple, the dining areas are really spectacular. There are several dining rooms, each done in a different color scheme and decor, and each beautiful. Many antiques are used, plus, of course, the ever-present tradition of fresh flowers enhancing every nook and cranny. The chef is famous for his culinary art and guests come from far and near to dine.

*Hostellerie des Chevaliers, Gruyeres*

*Medieval Villages*

Gruyeres is such a beautiful little town that it attracts bus loads of visitors who crowd the small main street during the day. However, most of the tourists leave at night and the town returns to its fairy tale quality. Return in the evening to the idyllic Swiss village and the town is yours to enjoy. Plan excursions during the day to avoid the bustle of the midday tourist rush. One possible outing would be to go to the small CHEESE MUSEUM just at the bottom of the hill from Gruyeres. Housed in a modern building, the exterior is painted with a pastoral scene and is difficult to miss. In the museum (which is also a cheese factory) demonstrations are given on how cheeses are made in the various Swiss cantons. There is also a movie, given in an English version, with an explanation of the process. Cheese enthusiasts might want to linger in this area and take more short excursions to visit other little villages and sample their dairy products...You might come home a little plumper, but a connoisseur of the marvelous varieties of the delicious Swiss cheeses.

*Castle of Chillon*
*Chillon*

Other sidetrips that might be appealing would be to travel the distance to LAKE GENEVA and explore the many quaint little towns along the lake. Of course, the ever-pleasurable rides on the lake can be picked up from most of the lakeside towns. From Gruyeres you can easily visit the famous CHILLON CASTLE located on a tiny peninsula near MONTREUX. This castle originally belonged to the Counts of Savoy but its great fame came from Lord Byron's famous poem "The Prisoner of Chillon".

When it is time to leave Gruyeres there are several options. It is just a short drive around Lake Geneva to GENEVA where there are train connections all over Europe plus international flights if you must return home. Or it is also a very easy trip to complete your "medieval" circle and return to Lucerne via the beautiful SIMMENTAL VALLEY, stopping along the way to visit the walled town of THUN.

# Best on a Budget

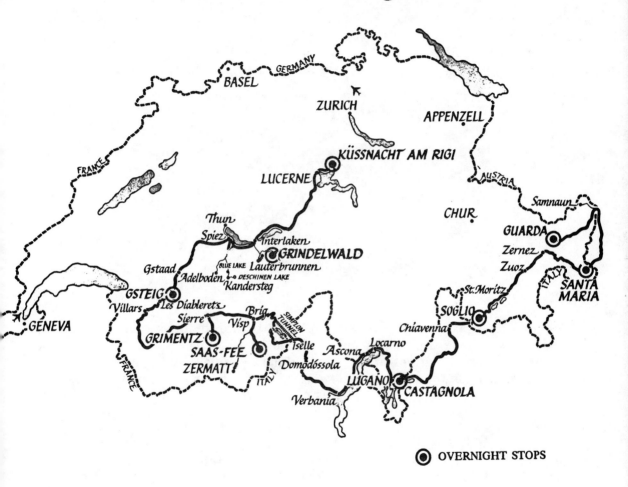

GERMANY

BASEL

ZURICH

APPENZELL

KÜSSNACHT AM RIGI

LUCERNE

AUSTRIA

FRANCE

CHUR

Samnaun

GUARDA

Thun

Zernez

Spiez

Interlaken

GRINDELWALD

Zuoz

BLUE LAKE

Lauterbrunnen

Gstaad

Adelboden

DESCHINEN LAKE

Kandersteg

St. Moritz

SANTA MARIA

ITALY

GSTEIG

SOGLIO

Villars

Les Diablerets

Brig

Chiavenna

GENEVA

Sierre

Visp

SIMPLON TUNNEL

GRIMENTZ

Ascona

Locarno

FRANCE

SAAS-FEE

Iselle

ZERMATT

Domodóssola

LUGANO

CASTAGNOLA

ITALY

Verbania

⊙ OVERNIGHT STOPS

# Best on a Budget

*Soglio*

This itinerary was almost never written. Just before the book went to press, we made a last-minute decision to include a budget itinerary, so it was back to the typewriter for some late-night sessions and here you have it: "Best on a Budget". What changed our mind was the following episode. Barbara Tapp, our illustrator, was studying photographs we had taken of Swiss hotels with the purpose of finding material to assist her with the hotel sketches. Coming across a snapshot of the Elvezia al Lago Hotel which we had put in the reject file, Barbara asked why we weren't including this "beautiful little lakefront inn". We carefully explained to her that the hotel was not quite of the calibre of the other hotels in the guide - it was just too "modest". The building was attractive but not an architectural masterpiece, the rooms were very clean but quite small. Barbara then asked the price.   It was extremely low.   "Oh, you must include it", she said.   "This is just the type of hotel my husband Richard and I would adore.   Our budget would stretch so much further.   We could stay a week with meals for what a few days would cost in some of the other inns for room only."   Barbara asked if we had others in the inexpensive category that were not going to be included.   Actually, we had been intrigued by several small inns found off the beaten path, such as the Hotel Palazzo Salis in Soglio, the Hotel Baren in Gsteig, and the Hotel du Moiry in the medieval village of Grimentz.   Barbara's enthusiasm for the qualities of these "little gems" was contagious.   So this itinerary is for my friend Barbara and for others, young at heart, adventurous in spirit and travelling on a budget.   Have fun.

## ORIGINATING CITY     KUSSNACHT     HOTEL DU LAC SEEHOF

*Hotel du Lac Seehof*
*Kussnacht am Rigi*

This itinerary begins at KUSSNACHT AM RIGI, a small village located on the northern tip of LAKE LUCERNE - a convenient spot to begin your journey as Lucerne is just a short drive away. For a change of pace and an alternative to driving, you might decide to take advantage of a ferry service between the two towns. The HOTEL DU LAC SEEHOF is situated right by the ferry landing and is managed by the fifth generation of the Trutmann family. The bedrooms are very simple, some quite small, but all immaculently clean and pleasant. The hotel has an inside dining room, but it is the lakeside terrace that is the choice for everyone when the weather is inviting. Here you can linger over a romantic dinner and know that the setting more than makes up for the fact that this is not a deluxe hotel.

## DESTINATION I    GRINDELWALD    HOTEL FIESCHERBLICK

The drive south from Kussnacht am Rigi to GRINDELWALD is beautiful. Perhaps the most spectacular portion is when you pass through the scenic area surrounding the famous resort of INTERLAKEN which is strategically located on a bridge of land connecting two of Switzerland's most beautiful small lakes, LAKE THUN and LAKE BRIENZ. At Interlaken you take a small road which branches to Grindelwald, only a short journey beyond Interlaken. The vistas are glorious as the road winds higher into the mountains and then dead-ends in a small town perched on a mountain meadow with glorious views. Your hotel for the night is the FIESCHERBLICK, which was originally the family farmhouse of the owner, Johannes Brawand. So many modern improvements have been made that the hotel does not look old, but it is, and vestiges of its origin can be seen in well-placed displays of farm instruments (family antiques now cleverly ornamenting the walls). The Hotel Fiescherblick is more expensive than the other hotels included in this budget itinerary. However, the price is a good value when you consider it includes breakfast and dinner. The reason we have included a stop in Grindelwald is because the train ride to the top of the Jungfrau (see page 33) is one of Switzerland's highlights and Grindelwald is a perfect place from which to begin this very special journey. If this stopover seems too extravagant, just bypass Grindelwald and continue directly on to the next destination, Gsteig.

*Hotel Fiescherblick, Grindelwald*

While staying in Grindelwald you will certainly want to include the Jungfrau excursion, but there are other wonderful possibilities for sightseeing in the area. With Grindelwald as your base, it is a short drive into Interlaken where you can meander through the town enjoying the ambiance of this Victorian-style resort. Better yet, take a lake excursion either on Lake Thun or Lake Brienz. Also highly recommended is a jaunt to see the medieval town of THUN with its dramatic castle perched on the hillside. A covered wooden staircase leading up to it adds to the fun of visiting the castle. If it is time to consider gifts, Thun has an interesting shopping street with a mall of shops on an upper level and an elevated sidewalk.

When leaving Grindelwald, wind your way back down to Interlaken and then head west on the road tracing the south edge of Lake Brienz.   Before reaching the town of SPEIZ, watch for a turnoff for a road heading south into the KANDERSTEG VALLEY.   This lovely valley is worth a short detour.   Beyond the town of REICHENBACH, watch for a sign on the right side of the road for the BLAUSEE (Blue Lake).   Park your car and follow the wooded, scenic pathway to this gem of a little lake with its curtain of rocks rising in the background.   One wonders how nature can compose such magic.   If you are ready for a snack, there is a charming little chalet-style restaurant nestled along the shore.   The Blausee is very popular and will be crowded if the day is nice - especially with families, since this little lake appeals to the little ones.   Continuing beyond the Blausee you come to the town of Kandersteg.   The road actually ends in this typical Swiss village with a splendid setting of meadows and towering mountains.   From Kandersteg you can take a chairlift to LAKE OESCHINEN, a beautiful high mountain lake surrounded by rocky cliffs.

After a stroll around the mountain village of Kandersteg, retrace your way to the main highway and continue west following the SIMMENTAL VALLEY toward GSTAAD.   Continue through the charming resort of Gstaad and in about 15 minutes you will come to GSTEIG which shares the same glorious valley as Gstaad, but not the same "jet set" prices.   Yet the town of Gsteig is is wonderfully quaint although without fancy restaurants.

When you reach Gsteig you cannot miss the HOTEL BAREN on the righthand side of the street near the small church.   The building facade is such a marvelous example of the intricate carvings characteristic of the Oberland region that the hotel is protected by the government as a "national treasure".   The town of Gsteig is custodian of the hotel and selects the management.   The dark wooden gables of the Gasthof Baren are covered in detailed designs and in summer the window boxes are filled with flowers, virtually a mass of brilliant red. The bedrooms are quite simple. If you want to splurge, one of the seven guestrooms has a private bath. The food has the reputation of being simple, but very good. The cozy dining room with its wooden tables and chairs and gay checkered curtains is a favorite with the locals who come to eat and drink.

*Hotel Baren, Gsteig*

Linger for a few days in Gsteig to enjoy the beauty of this tiny valley. There are many wonderful trails for hiking in the summer and in winter there is the world-famous skiing at nearby Gstaad. One day you might like to take a short excursion to the town of GRUYERES, a charming little "picture book" medieval village hugging the top of a small hilltop. The town is really only one main street full of picturesque buildings. Surrounding this "toy town" are incredibly green meadows which seem to flow up to the mountains - it is a scene for Heidi. The town is famous for its excellent cheeses and creams as Gruyeres is in one of the excellent dairy sections of Switzerland. If you go to Gruyeres be sure to stop at the Hostellerie St. Georges or one of the other restaurants for some quiche and, when in season, some berries with the unbelievably thick cream.

## DESTINATION III . GRIMENTZ HOTEL DE MOIRY

After leaving Gsteig, your next stop is the tiny town of GRIMENTZ. The drive from Gsteig to Grimentz is beautiful but involves mountainous driving and the route is only recommended after the snows have melted. As you leave Gsteig, follow the road which begins almost immediately to climb up into the mountains. The road twists over the mountains, passes through the town of LES DIABLERETS, the ski resort of VILLARS and then winds down into the Rhone Valley. Upon reaching the main highway turn east, and when you reach SIERRE, follow the signs for the road heading south to Grimentz.

The town of Grimentz nestles on a side of the mountain overlooking the valley and beyond to the high alpine peaks. The village is a masterpiece of perfection, with almost all of the buildings constructed in the traditional Valais style with dark weathered wood, slate roofs and balconies. All this is set off in summer by masses of brilliant red geraniums. The HOTEL DE MOIRY, found on the edge of town, is quite simple, but, for the location, an excellent value. The Grimentz area is

wonderful for high mountain walking.    It is possible to hike to neighboring villages.
If you become tired, or if the wine with lunch along the way makes you lazy, you can
always take the postal bus back to Grimentz.

*Hotel de Moiry, Grimentz*

## DESTINATION IV    SAAS-FEE    WALDHOTEL FLETSCHHORN

On the day of your departure, take time for a morning stroll or a leisurely breakfast
as the drive from Grimentz to SAAS-FEE is very short.    Return to the highway
that traverses the Rhone Valley and head east.    At Brig turn south towards

Zermatt and Saas-Fee.   Toward the end of the valley follow the signs for Saas-Fee. Here the road twists up the mountain and ends up at a parking lot for Saas-Fee where you must leave your car since the town is for pedestrians only.   Just opposite the parking area is the tourist office where there is a network of telephones with direct lines to each hotel. Call the WALDHOTEL FLETSCHHORN and advise them of your arrival.   Either Mr Dutsch, the owner, or one of the porters will come to meet you and whisk you off in their electric cart through the town, over the open meadow, then through a thick forest path to the Waldhotel Fletschhorn.   The first glimpse of the Waldhotel Fletschhorn will undoubtedly win your heart: what a sensational location.   The hotel itself is not the epitome of a small Swiss chalet - rather it is simply an attractive hotel, but the setting is incredible.   The hotel is located in a clearing of the forest in its own little world overlooking the SAAS VALLEY and the majestic towering peaks of the MISCHABEL mountain group.

*Waldhotel Fletschhorn, Saas-Fe*

110                           *Best on a Budget*

The Waldhotel Fletschhorn is not a bargain hotel in the normal sense. However, it is included because it really is a bargain when you consider the value received. First of all, is the gorgeous location. Second, the hotel has rates which include meals and so for the price of a hotel room alone in many of the fancy resorts such as Zermatt, at the Waldhotel Fletschhorn you have "room and board", and the food is some of the best in Switzerland. Irma Dutsch, who has the distinction of being the finest woman chef in Switzerland, not only oversees the preparation of the food, but actually is in the kitchen cooking each delicious meal. So when you make a reservation by all means sign up for demi-pension (breakfast and dinner) or better yet for full pension (three meals a day).

The third reason the hotel is such a great value is that your stay is also a social event. The hotel is almost like a house party where at the end of the day everyone sits around and compares their day's mountain adventures. In summer the conversations will share "favorite" hiking paths; in winter the talk will revolve around snow conditions and gorgeous views encountered on cross country ski trails. Your companions are likely to be guests very familiar with the area as the Dutsch family has, through their special gift of hospitality, built up a group of friends around the world who come every year. Large corporation presidents, lawyers, writers, Hollywood producers, etc. find their way to this simple Shangri La.

## DESTINATION V      CASTAGNOLA      ELVEZIA AL LAGO

If time permits, linger in the mountains at Saas-Fee. However when it is time to leave, rest assured that your next destination of CASTAGNOLA, although entirely different, is equally beautiful.

On the day of your departure, get an early start. The first leg of the trip is an hour's drive to BRIG and from there you have a choice of either driving over the

SIMPLON PASS or taking a train through the SIMPLON TUNNEL. Unless your budget is really slim, the train is by far the easiest way to cross the mountains and a fun adventure in its own right. If you decide on the train remember to allow enough time to purchase tickets and get your car to the designated boarding point. Directional signs are very explicit: they show a car on top of a train. The trains leave on the hour to travel through the longest train tunnel in Europe. You stay in your car during the trip and jostle in total darkness until you emerge approximately 20 minutes later at the town of ISELLE in Italy. Although there is a "short cut" to the Swiss-Italian lakes by following the turn-off near Domodossola through the Vigezzo Valley, I would suggest you stay on the main highway since the road is much better. Continue on toward VERBANIA and then follow the shoreline of LAKE MAGGIORE through the picturesque town of ASCONA (an excellent luncheon stop) and then via LOCARNO to BELLINZONA and then south via the freeway to LUGANO. Just a few miles to the east of Lugano, you reach the small suburb of Castagnola.

*Elvezia al Lago*
*Castagnola*

ELVEZIA AL LAGO, located on a foot path linking the towns of Castagnola and GANDRIA, is not directly accessible by car although you can take a car or taxi to a nearby parking area called *San Domenico*.   You also have the option of taking the ferry from Lugano and getting off almost in front of the hotel (boat stop is *Elvezia Al Lago*), but check the schedule carefully because there is not frequent service. One of our readers, who unfortunately had problems finding the hotel, kindly sent good directions if you are driving: "Leaving Lugano, take the highway toward Gandria, passing Castagnola and Villa Favorita (a lakefront museum in Castagnola).   Turn right on Via Cordiva (signposted *San Domenico*)."   The Via Cordiva deadends in the San Domenico parking area where you will find a phone booth.   From here, either call for the hotel to send their boat to pick you up at the adjacent dock or follow the footpath east to the hotel (about a 10-minute walk). The Elvezia al Lago is perched on the water's edge, easy to spot with its jaunty blue and white awnings.   This is a modest hotel, and although the guest rooms are quite small, they all have a view of the lake.   Best yet, in the morning you can awaken to the music of the birds, have breakfast overlooking the lake, and spend the day soaking in the gorgeous view.   Herbert Lucke (who speaks beautiful English) owns the Elvezia al Lago; he and his wife will do their best to see your stay is a happy one.   Unless there is a last minute vacany, you cannot make a reservation in advance during the busy season for less than several days.   However, this is not a problem - linger in the lake district for as long as time permits for there is truly so much to see and do.

From Castagnola take the boat into Lugano which still maintains in its central core a charming medieval village with excellent shops and restaurants or to the little town of MORCOTE and dawdle over lunch at the CARINA HOTEL'S little waterfront terrace. Another outing would be to visit the VILLA FAVORITA which you can either walk to from your hotel or reach by one of the ferries. The Villa Favorita is one of the finest private museums in Switzerland. Even if the displays were not so outstanding, the museum would be worth a visit on its own merits, for the Villa Favorita was formerly a gorgeous villa and its location is enchanting - along the shores of the lake surrounded by magnificent flower gardens.

## DESTINATION VI          SOGLIO          PALAZZO SALIS

If your holiday time has run out then you could conveniently end your vacation in Castagnola. You are just a short drive to the international airport at Milan or a pleasant train ride back to Zurich. However, if you can squeeze in a few more days there is high adventure ahead. In fact, the southeastern region of Switzerland (the Grison) offers some of the most spectacular scenery in the world.

Leave Lugano driving east into Italy. At the town of MENAGGIO turn north and drive along LAKE COMO. At the north end of the lake take the highway north toward the town of CHIAVENNA. The Swiss border appears just a few miles past Chiavenna and soon, high on a ledge to your left, you will spot the town of SOGLIO in the distance. This little town is one of the most dramatically beautiful in all of Switzerland, picture perfect - typifying the classic image of a Swiss alpine setting. A tiny village of just a few streets, the skyline dominated by a church spire, Soglio clings to a ledge high above the BONDASCA VALLEY and looks across to jagged peaks, whose moods are affected dramatically by the time of the day. Early morning light leaves a sliver of gold on the snowy escarpment enhanced by shifting clouds carressing the mountain peaks. The PALAZZO SALIS, a former mansion of the Salis family, a prominent family for centuries in the Grison, is now a hotel and marvelous value. Although the accommodations are extremely simple in their decor and most without private baths, the impression of an affluent era gone by survives with antiques in the public rooms. In the upper hall there are various shields, swords and portraits on display. The dining room is very attractive with mountain watercolors on the walls plus excellent food on the table. No one seemed to speak any English when I was at the hotel, but the graciousness of the owner, Mrs Cadisch, crossed the language barrier. With some sign language and a smile, communicating should not prove a problem.

*Hotel Palazzo Salis*
*Soglio*

Soglio is so spectacular that it deserves several days. There is not much to do in the village itself, but, if time affords, linger here, relax, venture on a hike or two and soak in the splendors and beauty of the setting.

## DESTINATION VII          SANTA MARIA          CHASA CAPOL

To leave Soglio twist back down the narrow road leading to the valley below and turn onto the highway in the direction of ST MORITZ. Famous first as a health spa, St Moritz is now considered the playground of the wealthy. From St Moritz continue north following the ENGADINE VALLEY. You will pass through ZUOZ, a small medieval village, along the way. Then head east from ZERNEZ where the road travels through the heavily forested SWISS NATIONAL PARK, over the OFENPASS and then down into the unspoilt rural beauty of the MUSTAIR VALLEY.

*Hotel Chasa Capol*
*Santa Maria*

Stretched along the sweep of the Mustair Valley are a number of unspoilt hamlets including SANTA MARIA which appears at the bottom of the Ofenpass. The HOTEL CHASA CAPOL is located almost at the eastern end of the town.

Dating back to the 8th Century, this little inn is truly unique: in addition to a hotel it houses a theater, chapel and a remarkable wine cellar. The hotel is owned by the Schweizer family who are involved in the management and supervision of the restaurant where dining and service are special. The bedrooms are simple in their decor, and, although rates are not as low as other hotels on this "budget" itinerary, they are an excellent value. The Chasa Capol is a delightful site for exploring the Mustair Valley and for taking advantage of the many miles of unspoilt trails in the nearby Swiss National Park.

## DESTINATION VIII          GUARDA          HOTEL MEISSER

When it is time to leave Santa Maria, drive east for a few miles to where the Mustair Valley flows into Italy and then loops back across the Swiss border. Following this suggested route saves backtracking along the same road. After crossing the border the route heads north just a few miles beyond customs and again across another border into Austria.

Shortly after entering Austria, the road travels back into the Engadine Valley and into Switzerland. This might sound confusing, but as you can see by the itinerary map very few miles are actually involved and it is an easy trip. The other advantage to this route is that it travels near SAMNAUN, a town near the Austrian border, soon after reentering Switzerland. Samnaun's biggest attraction is completely tax-free shopping. "Zoll Frei", the prices are incredible and people come from all over to purchase Austrian and Swiss clothing, hiking equipment and ski gear.

The final destination for this itinerary is in the UPPER ENGADINE VALLEY. Driving the valley from the east, you will pass the famous spa town of BAD SCUOL and then soon after the medieval town of GUARDA appears perched on a ledge above the valley, very similar to Soglio. The views are spectacular and the opportunity exists for some marvelous walks. Superbly situated on its own terrace overlooking the valley and mountains sits the HOTEL MEISSER - a modest hotel, reasonably priced, with a most attractive dining room and exceptional panoramas.

*Hotel Meisser*
*Guarda*

The main recreation in Guarda is enjoying the stunning views or hiking along one of the many easy trails. However, if you want to sightsee, TARASP CASTLE, picturesquely perched on a nearby hillside, has guided tours available in the summer months.

When it is time to leave this beautiful valley, it is an easy half day's drive either to Zurich or Lucerne.

# Switzerland by Train, Boat & Bus

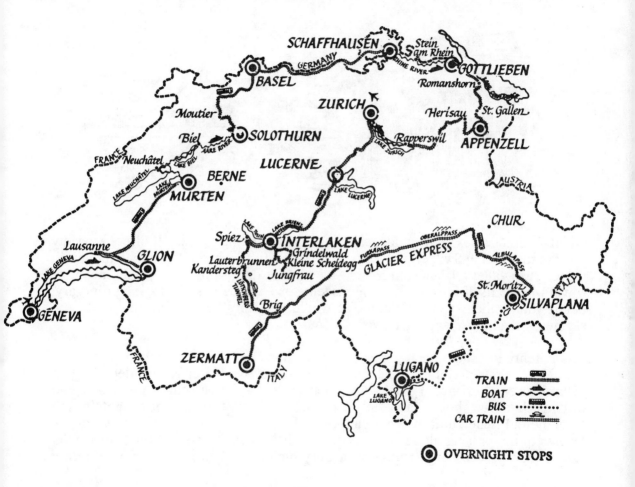

SCHAFFHAUSEN
Stein am Rhein
GOTTLIEBEN
GERMANY
RHINE RIVER
Romanshorn
BASEL
Moutier
ZURICH
Herisau
St. Gallen
Biel
SOLOTHURN
Rapperswil
APPENZELL
FRANCE
Neuchâtel
LAKE BIEL
AARE RIVER
LUCERNE
AUSTRIA
Lake Murten
BERNE
LAKE MUCHATEL
MURTEN
LAKE LUCERNE
CHUR
Lausanne
LAKE THUN
LAKE BRIENZ
Spiez
INTERLAKEN
OBERALPPASS
GLION
Grindelwald
Kleine Scheidegg
FURKAPASS
GLACIER EXPRESS
ALBULAPASS
Lauterbrunnen
Kandersteg
Jungfrau
LÖTSCHBERG TUNNEL
St. Moritz
GENEVA
LAKE GENEVA
Brig
SILVAPLANA
ITALY
FRANCE
ZERMATT
ITALY
LUGANO
TRAIN
BOAT
BUS
CAR TRAIN
LAKE LUGANO

⦿ OVERNIGHT STOPS

# Switzerland by Train, Boat & Bus

Of all the itineraries in the guide, this is the most exciting to me. It offers a variety of ways to travel in Switzerland from major cities to tiny hamlets via high mountain passes, lush valleys, lakes, and rivers - all without the use of a car. The means of travel weaves itself into the total sightseeing experience. This is a long itinerary, but if your holiday time is limited it would certainly be feasible to isolate the segments that most appeal to you.

The potential of this itinerary was realized when staying in Gottlieben, a town on the River Rhine. Noticing the ferry in front of the Hotel Krone departing to Schaffhausen, I wished I could just pick up my suitcase, climb on board and disembark a few hours later in front of another of my favorite hotels, the Rheinhotel Fischerzunft in Schaffhausen. How much more enjoyable to savor the lovely Rhine, passing along the way pretty little towns such as Stein am Rhein, rather than passing large trucks on a busy highway. The idea for this itinerary welled stronger a few days later when in Solothurn I was surprised to notice a boat connection to Murten, one of my favorite walled towns in Europe. How delightful, I thought, to journey through the countryside via canals and lakes instead of by car. So I returned home eager to see if the various travel segments by land and water could be coordinated. Knowing how remarkably efficient the Swiss transportation network is, I should never have doubted the feasibility of this itinerary. Although I have been everywhere mentioned in this itinerary, I have not yet had the fun of taking each of the boat connections suggested. But I will. This itinerary is planned for my benefit as well as yours.

This itinerary does have a few prerequisites. It is geared to a leisurely pace, so time must not be a problem: to hurry this particular holiday would prove frustrating and spoil the very reason it is special. Also, because some of the ferries operate only in the summer, vacation dates need to be carefully planned.

Finally, it is absolutely a must that you travel very lightly. I suggest just one tiny suitcase because cumbersome bags will be an aggravation and burden when trying to make quick connections between trains or boats, and certainly diminish some of the joy of travel. So pack lightly and join me in Switzerland by train, boat and bus.

*IMPORTANT NOTE:*

*In this itinerary I have given suggested times for the trains, boats and buses. These are to be used as a guideline only. You must check each of the schedules locally to verify times of arrival and departure. Some trains, boats and buses operate only on certain days of the week or during certain seasons of the year. Also, departure times can change. I debated whether or not to include the times and schedules, but decided that it was important to provide you with an approximate guideline so that you could basically see how the itinerary works and how it accommodates your own travel plans. However, again I want to stress that you personally verify schedules to avoid disappointment.*

*Hotel Les Armures*
*Geneva*

GENEVA, the first city on this itinerary, is a delightful starting point for a Swiss vacation.   Geneva is a lovely blend of the old and new - the medieval portion of the city rising on the hillside on the left bank of the Rhone and the newer city stretching out with peaceful promenades on the right bank of the river.   As you stroll the lake front of this international city you will hear languages from all over the world and see costumes of many nations.   In the spring Geneva becomes a small Holland with glorious tulips blooming in every little park.

The shopping in Geneva is wonderful - antique shops tempt the purse in the old section and the most sophisticated shoppers can find their haven in the beautiful shops and arcades in the newer section.

The HOTEL LES ARMURES is located in the old section of the city facing a tiny square.   If you enjoy a small, well run hotel without the crush of bus-loads of tour groups in the lobby, you will like Les Armures.   Even though the hotel was full when I stayed at the hotel, the lobby always seemed quiet and sedate.   To the left of the lobby is a lounge with antiques and comfortable chairs.   The bedrooms are not large, but are pleasantly decorated.   Request a room in the front overlooking the little park, if one is available.   The Hotel Les Armures is difficult to find since many of the streets in the old section of town are either closed to traffic or one-way. However, once you spot the spires of ST PETER'S CATHEDRAL, you will know your hotel is only a block away.   When you make a reservation, ask the hotel to enclose a map with directions to the hotel with your confirmation.

## DESTINATION I          GLION          VICTORIA HOTEL

The journey from Geneva to the next destination, GLION, is as much a sightseeing excursion as a means of transportation.   This is a glorious outing taking you from the western end of Lake Geneva to the eastern tip, stopping briefly in Vevey and Montreux before arriving at Terrietet.

9:50am      depart Geneva (Jardin Anglais pier) by boat
2:47pm      arrive Territet

Upon arrival in TERRITET take the little tramway which whisks you up the hill to Glion (the tram departs about every 15 minutes). Glion, a suburb of Montreux located high above the city, has spectacular views which is probably why there are so many elegant villas tucked in the trees overlooking the lake. One of these, the VICTORIA HOTEL, is set in its own beautiful gardens with a lovely vista over Lake Geneva. Staying here you will feel like royalty. The rooms have a variety of styles, but if you feel like splurging, ask for a suite redecorated in antique motif with a balcony overlooking the lake.

*Victoria Hotel*
*Glion*

*Switzerland by Train, Boat & Bus*

You might never want to wander from the beautiful gardens in front of the hotel. Here you can sit quietly on one of the strategically placed chairs and soak in the beauty of Lake Geneva whose deep blue waters are enhanced by the magnificence of the majestic mountains which frame her southern shoreline

## DESTINATION II    MURTEN    LE VIEUX MANOIR AU LAC

*Le Vieux Manoir au Lac*
*Murten*

Leaving Glion, your next destination is MURTEN. It is necessary to change trains several times, but the total travel time is short and the journey is beautiful.

| | |
|---|---|
| 9:43am | depart Glion by train |
| 9:55am | arrive Montreux |
| | |
| 10:09am | depart Montreux by train |
| 10:29am | arrive Lausanne |
| | |
| 11:14am | depart Lausanne by train |
| 12:21pm | arrive Payerne |
| | |
| 12:40pm | leave Payerne |
| 1:01pm | arrive Murten |

Your train stop is Murten, but the LE VIEUX MANOIR AU LAC is located about a half a mile south on the lake at MEYRIEZ. The Vieux Manoir Au Lac is an old manor house with a wonderful lakefront location plus excellent dining. Only a short walk from the inn, you enter through the thick walls into Murten and are magically transported back through the years to find yourself in one of the finest little medieval villages in Switzerland. Murten is like a living museum: as you meander through the little streets there are marvelous examples of medieval buildings, clock towers, ramparts, brightly painted fountains, and quaint little squares.

## DESTINATION III           SOLOTHURN           HOTEL KRONE

Today's trip from Murten to SOLOTHURN is like a treasure hunt as you weave your way by boat through the scenic lakes, canals, and rivers of the lovely Swiss countryside. Your adventure begins in the tiny walled village of Murten from where you take the ferry to BIEL to board the boat for the final leg of your journey on the Aare River to the walled city of Solothurn.

*Hotel Krone*
*Solothurn*

I stressed on the previous itineraries that time schedules *MUST* be carefully checked. Of all the destinations, this one is the most important because the boats basically operate only in the summer and *NOT ON MONDAYS*. However, if the boats do not operate to suite your time frame, it is always possible to make the journey from Murten to Solothurn by train. Another possibility, if you want to see the town of Neuchatel, you can make this a luncheon stop enroute to Biel if you leave Murten on an earlier boat. There are too many possibilities to mention them all.

| 2:45pm | depart Murten by boat |
|--------|----------------------|
| 6:00pm | arrive Biel |

The boat from Murten to Biel operates every day except Mondays from May to mid-October. At other times, you must change boats in Neuchatel.

| 6:05pm | depart Biel by boat |
|--------|---------------------|
| 8:20pm | arrive Solothurn |

The boat from Biel to Solothurn operates every day except Mondays during the months of July and August. In May and early September the boat operates only on Sundays. If your schedule does not fit into these dates, there are trains that leave about every half hour from Biel to Solothurn. A suggestion would be:

| 6:38pm | depart Biel by train |
|--------|----------------------|
| 7:07pm | arrive Solothurn |

How very appropriate when in the ancient town of Solothurn to stay in an old inn which perpetuates the mood of antiquity. The location of the HOTEL KRONE is perfect and so easy to find - facing a little square opposite the impressive ST URSUS CATHEDRAL

Solothurn is much larger than Murten, but also a marvelously preserved, completely walled medieval city located on the Aare River. It is fascinating to walk through this ancient town so full of the colorful atmosphere of bygone years. This town is so "perfect" that it was awarded the coveted Henri Louis-Wakker prize for excellence of renovations. From Solothurn you can also take a 35-minute boat ride along the Aare to ALTREU to visit the stork colony.

*Hotel Drei Konige am Rhein*
*Basel*

Your train journey today is short.

10:15am    depart Solothurn by train
10:45am    arrive Moutier

10:49am    depart Moutier by train
11:38am    arrive Basel

There is such a famous hotel in BASEL that it would be a shame to stay anywhere else. The HOTEL DREI KONIGE is one of the oldest inns in Switzerland, dating from 1026. This is also a very historical hotel, having been the site of the famous meeting between three kings (Conrad II, Henry III, and Rudolf II) who drew up the treaty for the transference of territories which are now western Switzerland and southern France. This historical meeting led to the name of the hotel "Drei Konige" which means "Three Kings".

The location of the Hotel Drei Konige am Rhein is terrific: not only can you enjoy watching the ever-changing drama of the river traffic passing by the hotel, but you are also only steps from the center of Basel. Although Basel is a large city, its heart is still a fun-filled medieval town of tiny squares, gay fountains, marvelously preserved old buildings, beautiful cathedrals, bridges, and many interesting museums.


DESTINATION V    SCHAFFHAUSEN    RHEINHOTEL FISCHERZUNFT

It is a simple and quick train ride from Basel to Schaffhausen:

  1:46pm     depart Basel by train
  3:01pm     arrive Schaffhausen

SCHAFFHAUSEN is another medieval town on the banks of the Rhine. So often in Switzerland one finds charming towns, but not a hotel to justify a stopover. Fortunately, this is not the case in Schaffhausen: the hotel here is so delightful that the hotel would almost be worthy of a visit even if the town itself were not an attraction. The RHEINHOTEL FISCHERZUNFT has an absolutely perfect location directly on the promenade on the banks of the Rhine.

*Rheinhotel Fischerzunft*
*Schaffhausen*

Just west of Schaffhausen is the famous RHEINFALL (Rhine Falls) which made it necessary for merchants to unload their river cargo and carry it around the falls before continuing their journey upstream. (The town of Schaffhausen grew up to service this river commerce.) If you have your own car, the falls are just a short drive from town; or, if you prefer, you can hire a taxi. But be sure to go - this waterfall is the most dramatic in Europe. You can view the falls from the shore or you can take a tour on a little boat which maneuvers right up under the giant cascade of water.

This journey along the Rhine is wonderful. It combines a splendid boat ride through quaint river villages with the practical aspect of getting between two delightful hotels. You can take a direct ferry which takes about four hours or you can get off the ferry in the fairy tale village of STEIN AM RHEIN to have lunch before boarding the ferry again for the completion of your journey to GOTTLIEBEN.

9:15am      depart Schaffhausen by boat
11:10am      arrive Stein am Rhein

Luncheon stop suggested in this picturesque medieval walled village

3:40pm      depart Stein am Rhein by boat
5:30pm      arrive Gottlieben

Hotel Krone
Gottlieben

When you arrive at Gottlieben your hotel is conveniently located just a few steps from the pier. The Schraner-Michaeli family owns the HOTEL KRONE and is very involved with its operation. The food is excellent and beautifully served in a cozy wood paneled dining room. There is also a cafe on the banks of the river for dining outside when the days are warm.

## DESTINATION VII          APPENZELL          HOTEL SANTIS

It is necessary to take a ferry plus several trains between Gottlieben and APPENZELL. It sounds complicated, but the Swiss in their predictable fashion have tailored the connections to work like a jigsaw puzzle - the connections fit together perfectly.

| | |
|---|---|
| 11:20am | depart Gottlieben by boat |
| 11:55pm | arrive Kreuzlingen |
| | |
| 1:32pm | depart Kreuzlingen by train |
| 1:57pm | arrive Romanshorn |
| | |
| 2:06pm | depart Romanshorn by train |
| 2:34pm | arrive St Gallen |
| | |
| 3:02pm | depart St Gallen by train |
| 3:48pm | arrive Appenzell |

In Appenzell the HOTEL SANTIS is located on a small square in the center of town. Typical of the style of the village of Appenzell, the Hotel Santis is gaily painted on the outside with decorative designs.

*Hotel Santis, Appenzell*

The village of Appenzell, a popular tourist destination because of its colorfully painted houses, is situated in a beautiful dairy farm area of Switzerland with soft rolling green hills dotted with enormous farmhouses that are a combination of home and barn. This is the Switzerland that every child envisions when reading "Heidi".

You can take a train from Appenzell to Zurich by making connections in ST GALLEN and WINTERTHUR, but it would be more fun to combine your journey into a sightseeing excursion. This trip will include the great beauty of the verdant Appenzell rolling green hills, the charm of the medieval village of Rapperswil, and the fun of arriving in the city of Zurich by steamer.

| | |
|---|---|
| 10:02am | depart Appenzell by train |
| 10:35am | arrive Herisau |
| | |
| 10:52am | depart Herisau by train |
| 11:39am | arrive Rapperswil |

You can make a direct ferry connection to ZURICH, but a suggestion would be to lunch in the medieval town of RAPPERSWIL with, if time allows, a visit to the museum in the castle which is perched on a knoll just above the center of the town. This museum contains, among other artifacts, a fascinating collection of Polish treasures brought to Switzerland for protection during World War II.

| | |
|---|---|
| 1:45pm | depart Rapperswil by boat |
| 3:40pm | arrive Zurich |

When you arrive in Zurich, it is about a ten-minute taxi ride to the HOTEL TIEFENAU, a most appealing, cozy hotel tucked in a small side street just a few minutes' walk from the heart of Zurich. The owners, Erica and Beat Blumer, are perfect hosts and the ambiance of their hotel is that of a private home. So, if you want to be away from the bustle of the center of Zurich and avoid the slick commercialism of some of Zurich's famous hotels, the Hotel Tiefenau makes an excellent choice - but you will need to book far in advance for this little charmer.

*Hotel Tiefenau*
*Zurich*

Although very popular with travellers from around the world, Zurich does not have the feeling of a tourist center. Instead, as you walk the streets you feel the bustle of a "real" city. Of course there are tourists, but shopping next to you in the little boutique will be the local housewife, hurrying down the promenade are businessmen on their way to work, and a couple from Zurich will probably be sitting next to you at a sidewalk cafe. Nevertheless, there is a carnival atmosphere to Zurich, a gaiety to the city. From both sides of the river the old section of Zurich radiates out on little twisting streets like a cobweb. Along the lakefront are parks and gardens.  From the piers there is a fascinating variety of boat excursions to little villages around the lake.  Being a large city, there is an excellent selection of museums to explore.


## DESTINATION IX          LUCERNE          WILDEN MANN HOTEL

A constant "commuter" service exists between Zurich and LUCERNE taking approximately an hour.  The trains usually leave a few minutes before each hour. When you arrive in Lucerne it is only a few minutes' taxi ride to one of our favorite Swiss hotels, the Wilden Mann.

*Wilden Mann Hotel*
*Lucerne*

The location of the WILDEN MANN HOTEL is fabulous - on Bahnhofstrasse, in the middle of the old section of Lucerne within easy walking distance of all points of interest.   The hotel embodies all that is best about Swiss hotels - the owner present to oversee every detail of management, excellent service from the staff, attractively decorated bedrooms, fine antiques liberally used in the public rooms, and one of the most picturesque restaurants in Lucerne serving delicious food.

Lucerne is a wonderful town for lingering: just strolling through the quaint streets and enjoying a snack in one of the small cafes overlooking the river can easily fill an afternoon.   There are always many tourists - Lucerne's enchantment is no secret. Everyone seems happy and there is a holiday air to the city.

| DESTINATION X | INTERLAKEN | HOTEL DU LAC |
| --- | --- | --- |

A frequent direct train service runs from Lucerne to INTERLAKEN, usually about every two hours.

| 1:22pm | depart Lucerne by train |
| 3:20pm | arrive Interlaken Ost station |

The HOTEL DU LAC is perfect for a train itinerary since it is located next to the Interlaken Ost (East) station.   Not only does this mean that when you get off the train you are "home", but also that when you get ready to take the spectacular JUNGFRAU CIRCLE, the train is at your front door.   When you arrive at Interlaken watch carefully for the train station.   The first station you come to, the Ost station, is the one you want.   Porters are usually right at the station to take your luggage to the hotel.

Situated on the River Aare connecting Lake Thun and Lake Brienz, the Hotel du

Lac is an attractive choice. The dining room windows open out onto the river where you can watch the boats and the swans drift by. The bedrooms are simple, but those that overlook the river have very nice views and some even have a small balcony. In addition to having a superb setting on a natural land bridge between the two lakes with a backdrop of majestic mountain peaks, Interlaken is famous too as the starting point for the Jungfrau excursion beginning at the Ost train station. On a clear day this train trip, which winds its way through the meadows and then twists its way to the top of the Jungfrau, is one of the most dramatic rides in Switzerland. (See pages 33-35 for details.)

*Hotel Du Lac, Interlaken*

Also, just steps from the hotel is the departure dock for the ferry boat which makes its way along the river and into Lake Brienz. Highly recommended is a trip on this ferry with lunch at one of the small villages en route before boarding again for the return to the Hotel Du Lac.

The OPEN AIR MUSEUM OF BALLENBERG is an interesting sightseeing excursion from Interlaken. Visiting Ballenberg is a wonderful way to learn about the various architectural styles and the crafts of Switzerland. This development reminds me of Rockefeller's preservation of the town of Williamsburg, reconstructing the crafts and style of living of the American heritage. This museum opened in 1978 and is still in the process of development. Do not wait for the completion because it will be many years before the dream of the whole project will be accomplished. Ballenberg is located in an enormous park like setting in a meadow above Lake Brienz. Houses, grouped according to region, have been brought to the park to show the most important forms of housing and settlement. Old ways of living and working and crafts are demonstrated and the interiors of the houses offer a glimpse into yesterday with their antique furnishings. To reach Ballenberg from Interlaken take the boat or train to Brienz. There are plans for a train from Brienz to the Park but for the moment you will need to take a bus from Brienz for the short ride.

## DESTINATION XI    ZERMATT    SEILER HOTEL MONT CERVIN

Your journey today will take you through some of the most spectacular mountain vistas in the world. How nice that you will be on the train and no one will have to miss the scenery because of concentrating on the road. This is an ideal trip by train since the section from SPIEZ to BRIG takes the "short cut" through the LOTSCHBERG TUNNEL which is for trains only. Also, the final leg of the journey must be done by train since no cars are allowed into ZERMATT.

| 10:25am | depart Interlaken Ost by train |
| 10:49am | arrive Spiez |

| 10:54am | depart Spiez by train |
| 11:59am | arrive Brig |

| 12:23pm | depart Brig by train |
| 1:45pm | arrive Zermatt |

*Seiler Hotel Mont Cervin*
*Zermatt*

There are no cars in Zermatt.  However, in true Swiss fashion, the problem of luggage and finding your hotel is easily solved.  When you arrive at the station your "coach" should be waiting.  The SEILER HOTEL MONT CERVIN has a stately horse drawn red carriage which will whisk you quickly through town to your hotel.  In winter the carriage becomes a romantic horse drawn sleigh.

The Seiler family is famous in Zermatt: they pioneered tourism in Zermatt with one of the earliest hotels, the Monte Rosa.  The Seiler family has continued in the tradition of caring for tourists and now owns several hotels in Zermatt, including the luxurious Mont Cervin located in the heart of town.  From the hotel you can saunter through the main street of boutiques or walk easily to the network of trails meandering under the face of the majestic Matterhorn.

## DESTINATION XII          SILVAPLANA          LA STAILA

Your trip between Zermatt and ST MORITZ is truly a "dream come true" for any train buff.   It used to be that you had to hip-hop across Switzerland changing trains at various stations to travel between these two famous mountain towns, but a few years ago an enterprising Swiss entrepreneur connected the two towns by a private railroad, the enchanting GLACIER EXPRESS.  You board the little red train in the morning in Zermatt at 8:54am (recheck the departure time since schedules change) and pull in to St Moritz station eight hours later, at 4:48pm.  It is necessary to make reservations in advance for the Glacier Express.  You can do so through the *FRENCH NATIONAL RAILROADS,* 610 Fifth Avenue, New York, NY 10020, telephone (212) 582-2110.  The Glacier Express chugs over some of the highest alpine passes in Switzerland, crosses meadows, tunnels through mountains, traverses glaciers, and weaves through canyons, all while you relax at your picture window.   There is even more if you plan ahead and make a luncheon reservation at the same time you book the train.   If so, you have the pleasure of dining in an old-fashioned dining car brimming with nostalgia - wooden paneled walls, bronze fixtures, tables set with crisp linens and fresh flowers on the tables. The train is expensive and not a part of the Swiss Rail pass, but the journey is a "train trip of a lifetime".

*La Staila, Silvaplana*

In the late afternoon the train arrives in St Moritz. Although there are buses to Silvaplana (about 15 minutes south of St Moritz), a taxi is the most convenient mode of transportation. LA STAILA, located in the center of the small village, is a simple hotel but appealing - especially attractive are some of the guestrooms in the older section which are beautifully paneled with old wood.

The final leg of your journey is by bus.   There is direct bus service from Silvaplana and reservations are necessary for this particular bus route.   Make them in advance at any of the postal bus stations in Switzerland.

2:47pm     depart Silvaplana by bus (reservations needed)
6:40pm     arrive Lugano (main train station)

*Hotel Ticino, Lugano*

When you arrive in LUGANO please get off at the central train station because from here you can take the little cable train right down the hill directly from the train station and almost get off in front of your hotel. If you have any questions about finding the funicular ask for directions at the tourist information center in the train station.

Lugano is a delightful city. Although it has grown tremendously, its core still has the atmosphere of a small medieval village. Right in the heart of the oldest section of Lugano is the marvelous little HOTEL TICINO, located on the tiny Piazza Cioccaro - a colorful square closed to automobiles. The Ticino (in days gone by a convent) is not a fancy hotel, but filled with olde worlde character and enhanced by the graciousness of its owners, Claire and Samuel Buchmann.

From Lugano you can either continue on into Italy for further adventures, or if you want to complete your "Swiss Circle" there is frequent direct train service to Zurich taking only about three hours.

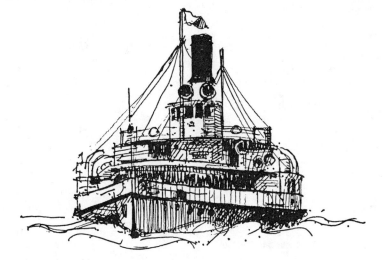

# Switzerland

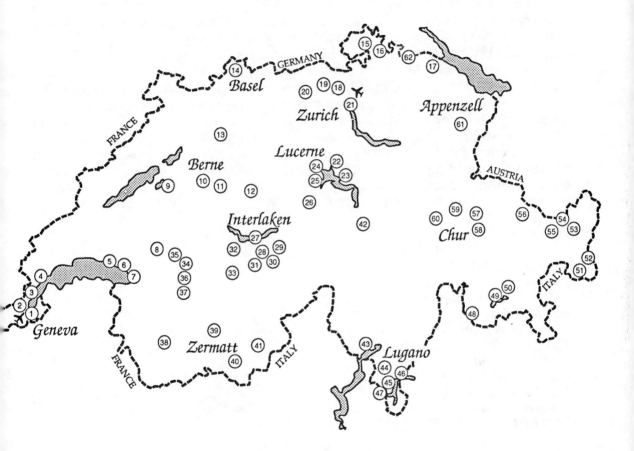

Map Showing Hotel Locations

147

On my first visit to the Star and Post Hotel my heart was won by Faro, an enormous Bernese mountain dog napping in the middle of the lobby. Faro was such a fixture that postcards of this gentle, affectionate overgrown "puppy" were sent to his many admirers. Unfortunately Faro has died, but Haro, an equally gentle, lovable Bernese mountain dog is winning the hearts of guests of all ages. The Star and Post has been in the Tresch family for several hundred years and Rosemary Tresch is the hostess, warmly greeting her guests. When first we met, I asked her if she were the owner. She replied, with a twinkle in her eye, that in Switzerland the woman is not the "owner", she is always the "owner's wife". The Star and Post Hotel's history dates back many years to when it was a strategic post station giving shelter to those going over the St. Gottardo Pass. About one-third of the rooms have an antique decor, but the majority are modern, so be sure to specify your preference at the time you make your reservation. The public areas abound with antiques and are very cozy.

*STAR and POST HOTEL*
*Hotelier: Familie Tresch-Gwerder*
*CH-6474 Amsteg, Switzerland*
*tel: (044) 6 44 40  fax: (044) 6 32 61*
*35 Rooms: Sfr 105-160*
*Open: All year*
*Credit cards: All major*
*U.S. Rep: Romantik Hotels*
*Rep tel: 800-826-0015*
*Old postal stop for St Gottardo Pass*
*Located 110 km S of Zurich*

The Hotel Santis is located on the central square in the picturesque village of Appenzell, the town of colorfully painted houses. The rooms are decorated in a variety of styles, my preference being for the rooms in the original part of the hotel which are decorated with copies of regional country style wooden furniture. I loved our room, number 42, which had a queen sized wooden canopy bed and a matching single bed. There was a nice desk and two chairs and, best of all, on the beds were blue and white checked comforters and plump down pillows. The public rooms seem geared to the influx of tourists who drop in for a midday meal, but the lobby offers a country welcome and the hotel has wisely insulated from the daytime activity a very peaceful and quiet lounge area. Joseph Heeb's pride and dedication as an owner are apparent from the friendliness of the front desk receptionist to the smile of the chambermaid, and, of course, the superb food in the dining room. The Santis has been in Mr. Heeb's family for several generations: it was owned by his grandfather and his father before him and since he has three sons and two daughters, the business will certainly continue to pass down within the family, hopefully for many generations to come.

*HOTEL SANTIS*
*Hotelier: Familie J. Heeb*
*CH-9050 Appenzell, Switzerland*
*tel: (071) 878 722  fax: (071) 87 48 42*
*35 Rooms: Sfr 120-180*
*Open: Feb to Dec*
*Credit cards: All major*
*U.S. Rep: Romantik Hotels*
*Rep tel: 800-826-0015*
*Located 100 km E of Zurich*

The Castello del Sole, situated within sprawling private park like grounds, has earned a five star rating and the acknowledgment of the Swiss government tourist office as being amongst the most deluxe hotels in Switzerland.   Located beyond the town of Ascona as you head east in the direction of Locarno, the Castello del Sole is bit difficult to find, but if you seek luxury and a place to be properly pampered, it is well worth the effort.   The Castello del Sole is graced with elegance and a subdued formality.   The atmosphere is set from the moment you enter the lobby and view the beautiful lounge areas accented with antiques and lovely paintings hung on pale colored walls.   From the public rooms to the comfortable spacious bedrooms, the decorating is delightful.  The Barbarossa restaurant maintains an exceptional reputation, specializing in using fresh products from the hotel's own farm and wines from its own vineyard.   The gardens of the Castello del Sole stretch down to a lake where the hotel has its own beach with small boats and wind surfers.   The hotel also has an indoor-outdoor swimming pool, sauna, five outdoor tennis courts and two tennis courts in a magnificent tennis hall which would fulfill any tennis buff's dreams.

*CASTELLO DEL SOLE*
*Hotelier: Mr B Kilchenmann*
*Via Muraccio 142*
*CH-6612 Ascona, Switzerland*
*tel: (093) 35 02 02*
*70 Rooms: Sfr 340-420*
*Open: Mar to Nov*
*Credit cards: None accepted*
*Tennis, pool, beach*
*Located 200 km S of Zurich*

The Hotel Tamaro, ideally situated across the street from Lake Maggiore, has cheerful little tables set out in front of the hotel attracting many who gather to enjoy a cup of coffee or an ice while leisurely watching the boats gliding in and out of the harbor.   As you enter the hotel the reception lounge, with an inviting array of comfortable antiques, is to the right.   To the left is one of the most charming features of this small hotel, an interior courtyard crowned by a glass ceiling for protection against the weather.   In this small inside patio tables are set gaily amongst many plants, giving the feeling that you are dining in a garden.   The guest rooms are situated on many various levels - sometimes it is like a game to find your room.   Although each of the bedrooms varies greatly in style of decor and size, they are all quite pleasant and immaculately clean.   I prefer the rooms in the front with a view of the lake - some even have small balconies.   However, the lakeside rooms are noisy, so if you prefer quiet, ask for a room in the back.   Annetta and Paolo Witzig are the owners of the Tamaro and they are very involved in the management of this delightful old Ticino-style patrician house: the charming and attractive Annetta is frequently at the reception desk greeting guests as they arrive.

*HOTEL TAMARO*
*Hotelier: Annetta & Paolo Witzig*
*CH-6612 Ascona, Switzerland*
*tel: (093) 350 282  fax: (093) 35 29 28*
*51 Rooms: Sfr 120-210*
*Open: Mar to Nov*
*Credit cards: All major*
*Across the street from Lake Maggiore*
*Located 200 km S of Zurich*

Although the spa town of Bad Scuol is a hub of activity, the Hotel Guardaval is isolated from the "action". Located on a road running above the highway, the hotel forms its own little world of tranquillity. Quite old, parts of the hotel date from 1691. The main building is simple in design - painted white with bright geraniums adorning the window boxes. The reception area and lounges, filled with antiques, lead off to the rear deck where tables are set for enjoying the sun and the spectacular vista. Stairs lead down to a lower level where there is a very large, especially attractive, dining room - airy and bright with light wooden furniture, heavy beams with intricately carved supports, and enormous windows to soak in the view of the mountains. An adjoining house, now turned into part of the hotel, is oozing with antiques - cradles, old clocks, sleds, beautiful country peasant style chairs, tables and copper set a perfect mood. Our room was in another annex located just half a block up the hill from the main hotel. Decorated simply, the rooms are very pleasant and the views are dramatic. Our corner room, number 66, had a bay window enjoying a delightful panorama of the valley below.

*ROMANTIK HOTEL GUARDAVAL*
*Hotelier: Mr P.A. Regi*
*CH-7550 Bad Scuol-Tarasp*
*Switzerland*
*tel: (084) 9 13 21   fax: (084) 9 97 67*
*45 Rooms: Sfr 140-200*
*Closed: April, May, November*
*U.S. Rep: Romantik Hotels*
*Rep tel: 800-826-0015*
*Located 220 km E of Zurich*

On a small side street, just steps from the tower through which you enter the medieval town of Baden, is the Hotel Zum Wilden Mann, renovated in 1986 within the shell of a 17th-century building. Upon entering, you climb a steep circular staircase to the second floor where on both sides of the corridor are the dining rooms decorated in an airy, light, modern motif. Up another set of stairs brings you to the third floor where there is a reception desk and several of the nine bedrooms. Although some of the bedrooms seem a bit stark in decor, guest room number 2 is delightful and worth the extra price. It is extremely spacious, with crisp white walls and furniture enhanced by an intricate wall painting which seems to have been preserved during the renovations. I am not sure if this is so, but definitely the ornate paneled ceiling, which blends wonderfully with pleasantly modern decor, is very old. The bathroom is large and modern and even provides robes for the use of the guests. Another particularly attractive guest room is number 3, a corner room which incorporates some of the original ornate columns into the decor. For a hotel in the heart of old Baden, the Hotel Zum Wilden Mann is a good choice.

*HOTEL ZUM WILDEN MANN*
*Hotelier: De Carlo Cosimo*
*Obere Gasse 33*
*CH-5400 Baden, Switzerland*
*tel: (056) 22 08 92*
*9 Rooms: Sfr 160-225*
*Open: All year*
*Credit cards: All major*
*Within walls of old city*
*Located 25 km W of Zurich airport*

The Hotel Drei Konige (Three Kings Hotel) originally bore the name "Zur Blume", "At the Sign of the Flower".  But soon after the inn was founded, an historic meeting took place between three kings: Conrad II (Emperor of the Holy Roman Empire), his son (who became Henry III), and Rudolf III (King of Burgundy).  At the meeting a treaty was drawn up for the transference of the territories which are now western Switzerland and southern France.  The hotel's name was then changed, understandably, from Zur Blume to the Drei Konige.  The Drei Konige is decorated with exquisite taste - formal antiques and lovely reproductions are found in the public and guest rooms which vary in decor, but are all attractive.  The bathrooms are generally large and equipped with many conveniences: enormous tubs, two wash stands, automatic hair dryers, giant towels and towel warmers. Rooms overlooking the Rhine warrant a splurge and the suites are spectacular, especially the Napoleon Suite, in regal shades of blue with an ornate ceiling - fit for a king.

*HOTEL DREI KONIGE*
*Hotelier: Paul Bougenaux*
*Blumenrain 8-10*
*CH-4051 Basel, Switzerland*
*tel: (061) 25 52 52  fax: (061) 25 21 53*
*90 Rooms: Sfr 290-420*
*Open: All year*
*Credit cards: All major*
*U.S. Rep: Leading Hotels of the World*
*Rep tel: 800-223-6800*
*On the banks of the Rhine*
*Located in heart of Basel*

Berne is a marvelously preserved medieval city, attracting many tourists who love to explore its many charming little squares and streets lined with picturesque buildings. Just on the edge of the town, within easy walking to all of the sights, is the Bellevue Palace which, although not a little inn, is divine. The decorating throughout sets an atmosphere of elegant sophistication. It has a dignified, formal entrance in subdued colors. The dining room is gorgeous, with rich wood paneling and tables set with crisp white linen, flowers and beautiful dinnerware. The lighting from wall sconces is soft and intimate. The bedrooms are spacious and tastefully decorated, individual in their style and color. The terrace at the rear of the hotel is perhaps what impressed me most: the view from the terrace is beautiful and here the formal mood vanishes as guests gather in this charming rendezvous. The Bellevue Palace deserves every star in its deluxe rating.

*BELLEVUE PALACE*
*Hotelier: Melchior Windlin*
*Kochergasse 3-5*
*CH-3001 Berne, Switzerland*
*tel: (031) 22 45 81  fax: (031) 22 47 43*
*158 Rooms: Sfr 370*
*Open: All year*
*Credit cards: All major*
*U.S. Rep: Leading Hotels of the World*
*Rep tel: 800-223-6800*
*Beautiful views from balcony*
*Located on edge of old Berne*

The Alte Rheinmuhle is actually in Germany, but for all practical purposes it is part of Switzerland since geographically it is like a small island of land, almost encircled by Switzerland.   Located only 4 km from Schaffhausen, the Alte Rheinmuhle is an old mill converted into a hotel, a truly wonderful transformation accomplished with delightful taste.   Even if the decor were not perfection, the site itself would overcome many faults.   The building dates from 1674 and sits right on the edge of the Rhine with the front of the hotel actually in the water.   As you dine, you can watch the river with its constant boat traffic intermingled with graceful, slowly gliding swans.   The hotel has earned an outstanding reputation for its cuisine and extensive wine cellar.   Some of the restaurant's specialties include superb venison, wild rabbit and the highlight for dessert is the most scrumptious cassis sherbet to be found anywhere.   I discussed the rooms with the management and was told that all rooms are decorated in a country style and furnished with antiques - some even have four-poster beds.  Request a room facing the river.  I cannot think of anything more romantic than enjoying a gourmet dinner in an enchanting restaurant, then climbing the stairs to be lulled to sleep by the Rhine flowing beneath your window.

*HOTEL ALTE RHEINMUHLE*
*Manager: Fredy Wagner*
*D-7701 Busingen, Germany*
*\* tel: (07734) 6076*
*\* German country code is 49*
*55 Rooms: Sfr 140-200*
*Open: Jan 10 to Dec 20*
*Credit cards: AX, DC*
*Positioned directly on the Rhine*
*Located 50 km N of Zurich*

When researching for the third edition of "Swiss Country Inns & Chalets" we wrote to each of the hotels already in our guide and asked if they could recommend other hotels of ambiance.   Two hotels wrote back about the very special Hostellerie Bon Accueil, so we went to Switzerland to see for ourselves, and our hearts were won. The Hostellerie Bon Accueil is just down the road from the famous ski resort of Gstaad, standing in a meadow above the village of Chateau d'Oex.   The inn, originally an old farmhouse, dates back 200 years, and although there have been many additions, the original chalet style is maintained with a long sloping roof, overhanging eaves and weathered wooden exterior.   Green shutters protecting windows accented with frilly white curtains add the final touch.   The bedrooms are individually decorated and - although simple - are attractive.   Comfy leather chairs and couches are used in the lounge and bar.   The furniture is mostly modern, yet touches of antiques maintain the cozy mood.   The dining room is especially inviting, with ladder-back chairs and wooden tables set around a brick fireplace. The hotel is renowned for its superb cuisine.

*HOSTELLERIE BON ACCUEIL*
*Hotelier: Antoine Altramare*
*La Frasse*
*CH-1837 Chateau d'Oex, Switzerland*
*tel: (029) 4 63 20*
*22 Rooms: Sfr 125-170*
*Open: Dec to Apr 15 & Jun to Oct*
*Credit cards: All major*
*18th-century farm chalet*
*Located: 200 km S of Zurich*

Every aspect of the Hotel Stern has been designed and managed with the guest in mind.   This is not a glamorous hotel, yet it is obvious that behind every detail is someone who cares and works very hard to achieve the greatest comforts.   Mr Pfister, the owner, is a true professional in his field.   He and his wife oversee every detail of management: Mrs Pfister is in charge of the housekeeping, bookkeeping and the hotel staff while Mr Pfister tends the front desk and is in charge of food and beverage and guest relations.   Located in the old section of Chur, the Hotel Stern dates back 300 years and is a wonderful blend of traditional decor and modern conveniences.   In the 20 years that the Pfisters have owned the Hotel Stern they have been dedicated to providing choice accommodations and an excellent restaurant, and they have done a tremendous job bringing this old hotel into the 20th century.   The bedrooms are simply furnished and comfortable, although not as attractive as the dining rooms and lounges which have more antiques.   The furnishings are principally of the light pine wood so typical in the Grison area of Switzerland.   The decor also profits greatly from the fact that Mr Pfister is an avid art collector and throughout the hotel are many skillfully displayed works of original art.   There is a wonderful collection of the paintings of the famous Swiss artist, Carigiet, whose whimsical scenes are inspired by his own childhood in a small country village.

Another interesting collection of the Pfisters' is a fabulous assortment of horse-drawn carriages and sleds stored in a garage behind the hotel.   The collection, which is like a tiny museum, ranges from simple country sleds to gorgeous carriages fit for nobility.   Mr Pfister's father owned these marvelous carriages for use in his profession as a driver.   Mrs Pfister told a wonderful story about her father-in-law who must be quite a man.   A few years ago, when in his seventies, he agreed as a favor to a friend to drive one of the carriages all the way to Germany for a political celebration.   En route he had an accident, was hospitalized, and ordered by the doctor to remain in bed and not continue the journey.   Undaunted, the senior Mr Pfister "escaped" from the hospital, caught up with his carriage, and arrived on time in splendor and style.   Any car buff would also envy a more modern counterpart, Mr Pfister's 1933 Buick Sedan.   With a brown exterior and dusty rose colored velvet interior, it is truly gorgeous and in mint condition.   As the city fathers were opposed to the use of horse stables in the town, the Pfisters instead use the Buick on special occasions.   On request, he can meet guests arriving by train.   (Note: speaking of trains, Chur makes an excellent choice for a town to stay in when either arriving or departing on the Glacier Express - one of Europe's most fabulous rail journeys.)

The town of Chur is one of the oldest cities in Switzerland and has many excellent medieval buildings.   A new addition to the town is a wine museum featuring an enormous antique wine press plus showcases displaying the history of wines.   Mr Pfister has been one of the sponsors of this extremely interesting museum and (with a little persuasion) can probably give you a short tour should you happen to arrive when the museum is closed.

*HOTEL STERN*
*Hotelier: Emil Pfister*
*Reichgasse 11*
*CH-7000 Chur*
*Switzerland*
*tel: (081) 22 35 55  fax: (081) 22 19 15*
*55 Rooms: Sfr 140-150*
*Open: All year*
*Credit cards: All major*
*U.S. Rep: Romantik Hotels*
*Rep tel: 800-826-0015*
*In heart of Chur*
*Located 120 km E of Zurich*

The Hotel du Lac is located on the lake only about 12 km east of Geneva. Although the hotel is directly on a busy road, behind the hotel is a delightful garden fronting onto the lake with the lawn stretching down to a private pier.   The Du Lac carries the air of an elegant home rather than that of a hotel.   It does not appear very old, but it is: in fact, in 1626 the Hotel Du Lac received the honor of enjoying "the exclusive right to receive and lodge people arriving by coach or horseback." At that time travellers by foot were excluded as guests of the inn because as a memorandum dated 1768 decreed: "The titled man of wealth riding in his own coach and four must not be housed with the peasant, the knife-sharpener, the chimney-sweep...the latter would feel too ill at ease."   The Hotel du Lac has been carefully restored and now you too can dream you are one of the guests arriving by "coach and four".   The hotel has retained many of its old beams, stone walls, and lovely antique furniture and artifacts.   All the bedrooms are attractive: some have kitchenettes; some have balconies with lake views; some have a small terrace squeezed into the jumble of tile roof tops.   For those who want to be away from the city, the Hotel du Lac makes an attractive choice for visitors to Geneva.   The hotel belongs to the prestigious *Relais & Chateaux* hotel group.

*HOTEL DU LAC*
*Hotelier: O. Schnyder*
*CH-1296 Coppet, Switzerland*
*tel: (022) 776 15 21  fax: (022) 776 53 46*
*18 Rooms: Sfr 170-220 (suites Sfr 330-800)*
*Open: All year*
*Credit cards: All major*
*Wonderful lakefront setting*
*Located 12 km E of Geneva*

The Auberge du Raisin is located in Cully, a sleepy little wine growing village. About a block from the hotel is a small park stretching along the shore of Lake Geneva - a perfect place to stroll while waiting for one of the steamers which pull into the dock tempting you to climb aboard to explore the lake.   The fame of the Auberge du Raisin is based on its reputation for serving exceptional food accompanied by the finest wines.   There are two dining rooms, each lovely.   My favorite, though, is the enchanting dining room just off the foyer: here you will find an oasis of gentle decor with cream colored walls, soft white draperies and white linen tablecloths draped across round tables spaciously set about on slate floors. Even the chairs, each stripped to a mellow light wood, maintain the "pastel look". Although the exterior of the hotel looks quite stern (a square box of gray relieved only by cheery red and white striped shutters) the interior of the hotel is delightful. Each of the guest rooms is pleasantly furnished in color-coordinated fabrics and maintained to perfection.   This small hotel, dating back to the 16th century, is a delightful choice while enjoying one of Switzerland's most charming wine regions.

*AUBERGE DU RAISIN*
*Hotelier: Familie Blokbergen*
*CH-1096 Cully, Switzerland*
*tel: (021) 799 21 31  fax: (021) 799 25 01*
*7 Rooms: Sfr 140-190*
*Restaurant closed Sundays*
*Closed: mid-Jul to mid-Aug, Christmas, Easter*
*Credit cards: All major*
*Gourmet restaurant*
*Located 70 km E of Geneva*

Dielsdorf is a small town north of Lucerne, only about 20 minutes by car from the Zurich airport or about 25 minutes from Zurich by train.   The hotel is owned by Christa and Eugen Schafer who also own the Rote Rose, a wonderful little inn only a few minutes away by car in the town of Regensberg.   The Rote Rose has only five rooms for guests and is frequently full, so it is nice to have an alternate choice for accommodation.   The Hotel Lowen, built in the 13th century, has been completely renovated.   The outside is painted white with small gables and shuttered windows enhancing the country appeal.   Floral paintings by Lotte Gunthardt, the world renowned rose artist, decorate the walls throughout this small inn.   The bedrooms are pleasantly decorated.   The suite is an especially large, light and airy room.   If you are on a budget, the guestroom without a private bath is a good value.   But the most attractive aspect of the hotel is the very cozy dining room.   Beamed ceilings, pretty linens, antique accents and fresh flower arrangements combine to create an inviting mood.   The food is excellent.   There are two choices of where to dine - either in the comfortable restaurant or the sophisticated tavern.

*HOTEL LOWEN*
*Hotelier: Familie Schafer*
*Manager: Urs Raschle*
*CH-8157 Dielsdorf, Switzerland*
*tel: (01) 853 11 32*
*19 Rooms: Sfr 90-160*
*Open: All year*
*Credit cards: AX, DC*
*13th-century inn*
*Located 20 km from Zurich airport*

The Hotel Adula, nestled in the woods above the mountain resort of Flims, is built in typical chalet style and, although it appears to be quite new, underneath the clever renovations the original hotel dates back to 1849.   This is not a small inn nor a simple inn.   The ambiance is one of elegance although the decor maintains a romantic country look.   The guest rooms are very pretty, reflecting a decorator's touch and enjoying every modern convenience.   Many of the guest rooms have balconies from which to enjoy the view.   There are two dining rooms: one is quite formal, the other (my favorite) is the "stubli", a smaller, beautiful wood paneled room, oozing with cozy appeal.   The emphasis is on fitness and the hotel offers many sophisticated facilities: swimming pool, sauna, solarium, ice bath, Turkish bath, gymnasium and massage room.   My preference is usually for smaller, less formal hotels, but for those who enjoy elegant surroundings and a wonderful selection of facilities, the Hotel Adula makes a good choice.   Adjacent to the main hotel and connected by an underground passageway is the Haus Soldanella, an even more deluxe small chalet superbly decorated in a country motif.

*HOTEL ADULA*
*Hotelier: Peter Hotz*
*CH-7018 Flims-Waldhaus*
*Switzerland*
*tel: (081) 390161  fax: (081) 39 43 15*
*109 Rooms: Sfr 210-290 (price includes 2 meals)*
*Open: mid-Dec to mid-Oct*
*Credit cards: All major*
*Swimming pool, sauna, 3 tennis courts*
*Located 150 km E of Zurich*

Le Richemond is situated on the Brunswick Garden about half a block from Lake Geneva.   It enjoys fabulous views of the Alps and the lake while having the added advantage of being off the noisy main street.   Le Richemond, founded in 1875, has been owned and personally managed by four generations of the Armleder family, accounting perhaps for the very personalized service which gives such a warm inviting air to this luxury hotel.   As you enter, there is a very attractive garden restaurant just off the lobby, and, on the left, a cozy bar with dark wood paneling. For gourmet meals there is an enchanting dining room whose richly brocaded walls and crystal chandeliers set the mood for intimate dining on tables beautifully dressed with the finest china and linens.   The guest rooms are decorated in a lovely traditional style.   For total pampering, the hotel has available a Rolls-Royce for sightseeing excursions.   Although not a country inn, for an elegant, charming hotel with a definite "olde worlde" flavor and a prime location in Geneva, Le Richemond makes an excellent choice.

*LE RICHEMOND*
*Hotelier: J. Armleder*
*Jardin Brunswick*
*CH-1201 Geneva, Switzerland*
*tel: (022) 731 14 00   fax: (022) 731 67 09*
*99 Rooms: Sfr 486*
*Open: All year*
*Credit cards: All major*
*U.S. Rep: Leading Hotels of the World*
*Rep tel: 800-223-6800*
*Elegant hotel near the lake*
*Located in heart of Geneva*

Geneva is known for its lovely lakeside hotels, but my heart in any city gravitates toward the old quarter where I can wander from the hotel and relive the magic of bygone ages.   Luckily, an appealing hotel exists in Geneva for those who, like me, prefer to be in the old section of the city.   I was immediately "taken" with the Hotel Les Armures from the first moment I walked into the intimate lobby.   There was no sign of any tour groups, only the presence of other guests sitting in a small lounge, talking quietly or reading - using the hotel as they would their home.   My room, number 202, had a queen-sized bed, a small round table accompanied by antique style high-backed armchairs, bedside tables with lamps, a small refrigerator and a very nice bathroom with a permanently installed hair dryer.   The room was quite small but very cozy with a beamed ceiling and wood-paned windows looking over a quiet shaded square and an old fountain.   I loved it.   When making a reservation, I would definitely request a room overlooking the square - also, since the hotel is difficult to find, ask the hotel to send you their map with instructions on how to get to the hotel.

*HOTEL LES ARMURES*
*Hotelier: Amedee Granges*
*1 Rue du Puits St Pierre*
*CH-1204 Geneva, Switzerland*
*tel: (022) 28 91 72  fax: (022) 28 98 46*
*28 Rooms: Sfr 320-400*
*Open: All year*
*Credit cards: All major*
*U.S. Rep: Jacques de Larsay*
*Rep tel: 800-223-1510*
*Located in old section of Geneva*

The Hotel Victoria, which looks like a stately French manor, enjoys a prime location in a park like setting in the suburb of Montreux called Glion, perched in the hills above the city.   As you walk inside, the first impression of the hotel is set by a rather dark and formal reception area.   However, as you continue the hotel opens onto some charming lounges.   One of my favorite rooms is the cheerful, bright, garden "sun room", a delightful spot to enjoy a good book or afternoon tea. The bar area is cozy, with dark paneling enhanced by old paintings, and there are two beautifully decorated dining rooms.   The cuisine is delicious and the manager, Mr Mittermair, is like a host in a private home, mingling throughout the dining room at dinner time to make sure that all his guests are cared for and happy. Some of the rooms are beautifully decorated with fine antique reproductions and have a glorious view stretching across the town of Montreux, over the lake to the mountains beyond.   Request one of the rooms which have been renovated because the others are a bit stuffy.   Also, you must request a room with a view - it is well worth the extra cost.   The Victoria belongs to the prestigious *Relais & Chateaux* hotel group.

*HOTEL VICTORIA*
*Hotelier: Toni Mittermair*
*CH-1823 Glion, Switzerland*
*tel: (021) 963 31 31  fax: (021) 963 13 51*
*40 Rooms: Sfr 200-260*
*Open: All year*
*Credit cards: All major*
*Swimming pool*
*Gorgeous views over Lake Geneva*
*Located 90 km E of Geneva*

With the River Rhine directly in front narrowing to connect with Lake Constance, the setting of the Hotel Krone is truly idyllic. An intimate terrace occupies the water's edge and in good weather is set with an inviting cluster of dining tables. When first I visited the Hotel Krone, I fell in love with this beautiful small hotel and with the gracious Schraner-Michaeli family who personally pamper each guest. The ambiance of the dining room is most appealing: fresh flowers are lavishly used and the paneling and furnishings are beautiful. Best yet, the food is exceptional. I am happy to be able to report that on our recent visit, all of the bedrooms had been refurbished and are most attractive. If you want to splurge, there are two mini-suites facing the river decorated in ornate antiques. The Hotel Krone makes an excellent base for exploring the northern region of Switzerland and just steps from the door you can board the ferry which will take you along the Rhine. On a day's boat excursion you can visit the delightful village of Stein am Rhine with its wonderfully painted buildings or the medieval town of Schaffhausen.

*HOTEL KRONE*
*Hotelier: George Schraner-Michaeli*
*CH-8274 Gottlieben, Switzerland*
*tel: (072) 69 23 23  fax: (072) 69 24 56*
*22 Rooms: Sfr 170-230*
*Open: All year*
*Credit cards: All major*
*U.S. Rep: Romantik Hotels*
*Rep tel: 800-826-0015*
*Wonderful position on the Rhine*
*Located 67 km NE of Zurich*

Sometimes I will include a town because of an inn's location, but, in this case, I've included an inn because I fell in love with the town. The mountain village of Grimentz is a bundle of old, storybook, darkened-wood-timbered chalets, brilliantly accented with colorful flowers. This village deserves to be explored and its appeal demands that you linger. Tucked at the entrance to the village is a pretty little whitewashed inn, with handsome wood shutters. When we originally visited the Hotel de Moiry, the bedrooms were quite simple and only a few had the luxury of a private bathroom. But now all have been renovated in a cozy, wood-paneled style and each has a private bath. Marvelous sunshine blessed our visit and we were able to dine on the patio in front of the hotel enjoying a memorable meal of fondue, salad, crusty, dark bread and beer. The dining room inside is warmed by a cozy fireplace, and the tables are set with fresh cloths and flowers. Be sure to notice a mural on one of the walls which portrays an annual competition between the cows of the area to determine the leader. (I am happy to report that the cows belonging to the Hotel de Moiry are consistently the winners.)

*HOTEL DE MOIRY*
*Hotelier: Aurel Salamin*
*CH-3961 Grimentz*
*Switzerland*
*tel: (027) 65 11 44*
*16 Rooms: Sfr 80-94*
*Open: All year*
*Credit cards: All Major*
*Charming high mountain village*
*Located 200 km E of Geneva*

Overlooking the lovely little Grindelwald church is the small, shuttered chalet-style Hotel Fiescherblick.  The hotel is not fancy but does possess a most inviting atmosphere.  As you enter the lobby the mood is set by a great old Swiss clock, a painted Swiss wall cupboard, a little table joined by a regional alpine chair and a few very old milking stools.  The dining room is decorated with modern furniture but the flowers on the tables, and the pewter mugs and antiques that adorn the walls add warmth to the area.  (The food is quite well known locally).  In addition to the main room, there is an outdoor restaurant at street level.  A small terrace, one level up, is reserved for the use of hotel guests only.  I was intrigued with the many little niches throughout the hotel artistically displaying antique farm implements. Mr Brawand explained that the inn was originally his family's home and the collection of various farm tools were used on his father's farm.  In one area are a number of cheese-making utensils, churns, a milking stool, the sieves and the wooden frames.  Upstairs the "olde worlde" feeling vanishes, but the rooms are clean and tidy.  Some of the bedrooms have a small balcony and the views are so startling that the simplicity of the rooms, by contrast, seems only appropriate.

*HOTEL FIESCHERBLICK*
*Hotelier: Mr Johannes Brawand*
*CH-3818 Grindelwald, Switzerland*
*tel: (036) 53 44 53   fax: (036) 53 44 57*
*23 Rooms: Sfr 114-160*
*Closed in Nov*
*Credit cards: All major*
*Gorgeous mountain views*
*Located 190 km S of Zurich*

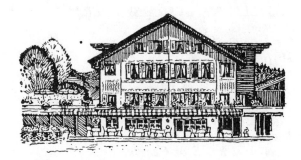

The Hostellerie des Chevaliers is located in the hilltop medieval village of Gruyeres, and is easy to find on the hill above the central parking area. As you climb up to the hotel, you come upon a delightful patio where white lawn chairs are strategically placed for guests to soak in the beautiful mountain view. The guest rooms are not elegant, but are quite attractive. They have a country feeling with simple wooden furniture and freshly painted white walls. Be sure to request one of the rooms in the back - these have a stunning unobstructed view over the rolling hills and up to the high mountains. The Hostellerie des Chevaliers is renowned for its cuisine which is beautifully served in delightful surroundings. Adjacent to the guest rooms is a separate building which hosts a series of charming, intimate dining rooms: country antiques fill the rooms; copper hangings and country, blue and white tiles adorn the walls; the floors are laid in handsome tiles; masses of beautiful flower arrangements are found everywhere. The rhythmic ticking of an old grandfather clock escapes from one of the dining rooms, setting quite a romantic mood. The Hostellerie des Chevaliers is a member of the prestigious *Relais & Chateaux* hotel group.

*HOSTELLERIE DES CHEVALIERS*
*Hotelier: G. & S. Bouchery*
*CH-1663 Gruyeres, Switzerland*
*tel: (029) 6 19 33*
*34 Rooms: Sfr 125-210*
*Open: Feb 15 to Oct 1*
*Credit cards: All major*
*Adjacent to medieval walled village*
*Beautiful mountain views*
*Located 92 km E of Geneva*

The Hostellerie de St Georges is a simple hotel ideally located at the heart of the marvelous little medieval village of Gruyeres. The hotel is named for old St George himself, and you will see our mighty hero slaying the dragon on the brightly colored emblem proudly displayed over the front door and again on a carving hung over an antique chest in the main hallway. Each bedroom is not only numbered, but also has a motif from the era of St George. As an example, on the door of one room there is a whimsical knight with a sword raised high, on another a musician playing an instrument similar to a bagpipe, while yet another has a witch-like character riding a broom. Each bedroom is similar in size and decor. Although the bedrooms are simple, the dining room is very attractive and when the weather is friendly, there is an outside terrace with a stunning view over the valley. The food cannot be described as anything but superb. Gruyere cheese, famous the world over, is served at every meal and the Gruyere cheese quiche of the hotel is so incomparably light, with such a delicate pastry, that it is tempting to order it at every meal. Our visit fortunately coincided with strawberry season, and so our dinner concluded with a large bowl of fruit smothered in the thickest cream I had ever seen - another product of the clever Gruyeres cows.

*HOSTELLERIE DE ST GEORGES*
*Hotelier: Mr Heribert Miedler*
*CH-1663 Gruyeres, Switzerland*
*tel: (029) 6 22 46  fax: (029) 2 38 23*
*14 Rooms: Sfr 128-192*
*Open: Mar to Nov*
*Credit cards: All major*
*Center of medieval Gruyeres*
*Located 92 km E of Geneva*

Located on the main street in the heart of the quaint mountain village of Gstaad, the Hotel Olden is quite famous.   Especially well known are its three restaurants - so well known that visiting dignitaries and movie stars frequent them when in Gstaad.   The restaurant situation at the Hotel Olden is quite unique because under one roof gather all the local farmers and workmen who come to the old pub, "Pinte", and also the jet-set of the world who come to dine and dance in the other very chic restaurants.   The menu is superb and includes many regional favorites such as delicious fondues and scrumptious desserts such as Gletscherkuss (ice cream and cherries flambe).   The outside of the Hotel Olden is of a chalet style with cream colored facade and green shutters and of course in summer the ever-present colorful flower boxes.   In addition there are regional Bernese designs painted on the front of the building to accentuate the windows.   The bedrooms have all been renovated and have an extremely personal touch in that much of the furniture and walls has been painted delicately by the owner, Heidi Donizetti, in typical Swiss country designs.   Even if you do not stay at the Hotel Olden while in Gstaad, stop by for a meal and look around.   Who knows, at the next table might be Audrey Hepburn or Roger Moore.

*HOTEL OLDEN*
*Hotelier: Heidi Donizetti*
*CH-3780 Gstaad, Switzerland*
*tel: (030) 4 34 44  fax: (030) 4 61 64*
*15 Rooms: Sfr 168-252 (summer)*
*Open: All year except May*
*Credit cards: All major*
*Swimming pool*
*Located 190 km W of Zurich*

The Post Rossli is an appealing small hotel in the heart of the pretty town of Gstaad. Little touches show a special personal touch. There are plants in the entry and a few well placed antiques to give an inviting welcome, and off the hall are two marvelous dining rooms. One tends to be used for the casual lunch hour. The other is truly charming, with wood paneling, alpine style chairs carved with heart designs and tied merrily with red cushions, green plants, some old prints, and copper pieces displayed on the walls. Like the decor, the cuisine is exceptional. The bedrooms have recently all been refurbished (some of them in very old wood) and equipped with every comfort including TV, mini bars and direct-dial phones in every room. Some of the rooms have their own balcony or porch, but since the hotel is located in the center of town the views are not spectacular. Gstaad is a busy tourist town, but the country village aspect has not gone, as we discovered upon awaking to the sound of melodic cow bells instead of the noise of traffic: out of the window we saw a herd of cows whose pace was governed by the singsong chant of a young boy. Mr Widmer, the owner, not only acts as the gracious host, but in the summer he can serve the guests as a trail guide and in the winter as a ski guide.

*POST HOTEL ROSSLI*
*Hotelier: Mr Ruedi Widmer*
*CH-3780 Gstaad, Switzerland*
*tel: (030) 4 34 12*
*21 Rooms: Sfr 140-210*
*Closed: Nov and mid-May to mid-June*
*Credit cards: All major*
*Chalet style inn*
*Located 190 km W of Zurich*

The Alpenrose was closed between seasons when I visited the Gstaad area, but I called ahead, and the owner, Monika Von Siebenthal, graciously offered to meet me at the inn and give me a personal tour.   It was snowing when I arrived, and Monika appeared at the same time, walking briskly up the road, warmly dressed in boots and cap with her enormous, lovable dog "Sammy" in tow.   Although the inn was in the midst of "Spring cleaning", I saw all of the guest rooms and had the opportunity to become friends with Monika, a very special person - young, pretty and filled with a gracious warmth.   Monika, with the support of her five children, runs the Alpenrose.   She personally assists in the decor of each of the rooms and her loving "touches" are everywhere.   One of the sons, having graduated from hotel school, assists in maintaining the excellence of the kitchen.   When I first visited, there were only 5 guest rooms, but Monica told me of her plans to add onto the tiny inn.   Finally permission to build has been granted and as this book goes to press, 15 additional rooms are being completed.   Monika tells me they will have the same individual country ambiance as the ones I saw plus each will have a lovely view balcony.   There is also a large deck - capturing the sensational mountain vistas and the sun.

*HOTEL ALPENROSE*
*Hotelier: Monika Von Siebenthal*
*CH-3778 Gstaad-Schonried, Switzerland*
*tel: (030) 4 67 67  fax: (030) 4 67 12*
*20 Rooms: Sfr 120-300*
*Closed: Nov and May*
*Credit cards: VS, DC, EC*
*Small, family-owned chalet*
*Located 180 km W of Zurich*

Although at first inspection the Hotel Ermitage-Golf Solbad appears to be a modern resort, it is actually a very old inn.   Only the heart of the hotel is the original small wooden house - almost hidden now by the modern new wings. However, the exterior is in keeping with the traditional chalet style, architecturally preserving the atmosphere of the original building.   Inside the hotel remains very wonderful, very old, very Swiss.   An inviting lounge area is warmed by a fireplace and the dining room is beautifully paneled and enhanced by crisp white curtains, white table linens and cheerful flower arrangements.   The bedrooms are modernly furnished, and if you are able to reserve a room with a view, you will be afforded a splendid unobstructed panorama of the gorgeous Swiss Alps rising across the meadow.   The Ermitage Golf-Solbad has so many modern amenities (a sauna, fitness/massage center, squash, tennis courts) that in a way I hesitated to recommend it for fear that it far exceeded the definition of "country inn", but after a long day of sightseeing, I found the facilities a welcome bonus.

*HOTEL ERMITAGE-GOLF SOLBAD*
*Hotelier: H. Lutz*
*Manager: L. Schmid*
*CH-3778 Gstaad-Schonried*
*Switzerland*
*tel: (030) 4 27 27  fax: (030) 4 71 95*
*72 Rooms: Sfr 260-380 (with 2 meals)*
*Open: May to Nov & Dec to Apr*
*Credit cards: AX, VS, DC*
*Swimming pool, tennis, golf*
*Located 180 km W of Zurich*

We were exploring the valley beyond Gstaad, heading south toward the soaring mountains, when we discovered the picture book-perfect hamlet of Gsteig.  In the middle of the village near the church is the Hotel Baren with what must be one of the prettiest facades in Switzerland.  The Hotel Baren is what is termed a typical Saanen-style house and this original 17th-century wooden inn is such an outstanding specimen it is protected under special Swiss law.  The heavy, sculptured beams and intricately carved exterior walls are exquisite.  In summer the cheerful geraniums at each window, red checked curtains peeking through the small window panes, plus the jaunty Swiss flags hanging from the upper windows enhance the image of the perfect Swiss inn.  The decor in the dining room continues with the regional flavor.  This cozy room is richly paneled and furnished with country style wooden chairs and tables.  Red checked tablecloths and fresh flowers on the tables add further charm.  The inn is largely famous for its cuisine. However, there are several very simple, moderately decorated bedrooms whose beds are decked with inviting traditional soft, down comforters.  When requesting a room, please note that only one guest room has a private bath.

*HOTEL BAREN*
*Hotelier: Familie B. Ambort*
*Manager: Sonja Ambort*
*Ch-3785 Gsteig, Switzerland*
*tel: (030) 5 10 33*
*7 Rooms: Sfr 85-105*
*Closed: Nov*
*Credit cards: All major*
*Located 170 km E of Geneva*

Clinging to a narrow shelf, the old town of Guarda seems to reach out precariously over the Unter-Engadin valley.   The day was gloriously sunny and warm, a moment of autumn perfection, as we entered this town of twisting streets, characteristic old homes colored with flower boxes at every window, intricately carved old hay barns and spectacular views.   Influenced by this absolutely magnificent day, I was in the mood to find a gem of a hotel to match the charm of the village.   Almost the first hotel I saw was the Hotel Meisser, beautifully situated on a promontory overlooking the expanse of green valley below.   On the lawn were tables set in the warm sunshine while waitresses in bright alpine costumes were busy serving the happy guests.   I could not have imagined a more blissful scene.   Although the hotel does not appear to be extremely old, it does have some antiques used throughout the public areas and pieces of old copper, baskets of flowers and heavy chests to add further cozy touches.   The dining room is especially appealing with large windows capturing a splendid view of the mountain vista.   Most of the guest rooms have recently been redone with beautiful wallpaper and country-style curtains.   Several of the guest rooms are especially outstanding with wonderful mellow wood paneling and country antique furniture.

*HOTEL MEISSER*
*Hotelier: Ralf Meisser*
*Ch-7549 Guarda, Switzerland*
*tel: (084) 9 21 32   fax: (084) 9 24 80*
*25 Rooms: Sfr 120-160*
*Open: Jun to Oct*
*Credit cards: DC, AE, VS*
*Marvelous mountain village*
*Glorious views from terrace*
*Located 210 km E of Zurich*

Encountering heavy traffic as we drove south toward the Hotel Waldhaus, we longed to return to the peace and quiet of rural Switzerland.   Therefore we were very pleased to find that Horw, although only a short distance in miles, is far removed in mood from the city of Lucerne.   The Hotel Waldhaus, situated in the gentle hills above Horw, resembles a country manor.   This appealing inn is owned by the gracious Kurt and Marlise Buholzer.   Their love of horses is apparent throughout the hotel: as we climbed the stairs to our room (spacious and pleasantly furnished), there were prints of numerous race horses decorating the walls along the staircase.   Looking out through the large windows of our room to the terrace below, we observed a number of guests lounging in their jodhpurs enjoying drinks in the late afternoon sun with only the pleasant sound of horses returning to their stables breaking the countryside silence.   We couldn't help feeling as if we had just arrived at an elegant estate and joined a private house party, a party given by the "horsy set" of the landed gentry.   Dining is also very reminiscent of being in a private home.   There is not one room but several formal, elegant, intimate dining areas each with windows looking out across the patio and beyond to a wide expanse of countryside vistas.   The setting is lovely: on a clear day you can set the lake and mountains from the terrace.   The Hotel Waldhaus is a member of the prestigious *Relais & Chateaux* hotel group

*HOTEL WALDHAUS*
*Hotelier: Kurt Buholzer*
*CH-6048 Horw-Oberruti, Switzerland*
*tel: (041) 47 17 54  fax: (041) 47 27 29*
*17 Rooms: Sfr 140-190 (Suites Sfr 240-280)*
*Open: All year*
*Credit cards: All major*
*Countryside manor*
*Located 10 minutes S of Lucerne*

The Hotel du Lac, owned by the Hofmann family for over 100 years, is more French than Swiss in appearance, with a gray mansard roof and pink facade.   The hotel is superbly located, directly on the banks of the Aare River as it flows between the two lakes of Brienz and Thun.   Many of the bedrooms overlook the river - a peaceful scene of boats and swans gliding below the window.   Since my last visit, Ernst Hofmann says that the hotel has completed the refurbishing of its 40 guest rooms and all now offer modern comfort and stylish decor.   There are two dining rooms: one is especially appealing, with large windows that open onto lovely river views. If you come to the Hotel du Lac expecting a charming little country inn, you will be disappointed, but if you enjoy a hotel with antiquated charm and personalized management, you will be content.   Most important of all is the Hotel Du Lac's location: just steps from where the train departs for the Jungfrau excursion and minutes from the dock where the boat leaves for Lake Brienz.

*HOTEL DU LAC*
*Hotelier: Familie Hofmann*
*Hoheweg 225*
*CH-3800 Interlaken, Switzerland*
*tel: (036) 22 29 22*
*Open: All year*
*40 Rooms: Sfr 155-190*
*Credit cards: AE, VS, MC*
*U.S. Rep: Best Western*
*Rep tel: 800-528-1234*
*Adjacent to train for Jungfrau trip*
*Located 175 km S of Zurich*

The grandeur of the Victoria Jungfrau is famous throughout the world. Mr Edouard Ruchti, a member of the Swiss Federal Parliament, commissioned the building of the hotel in 1864, and its exclusive design was dictated by the clientele he intended to attract. Although it was hoped that Queen Victoria might one day grace the guest list (a hope reflected in the hotel's name) she never managed a trip to Interlaken. The Victoria Jungfrau is one of Switzerland's most deluxe hotels: the service is refined and faultless. Elegance captivates the atmosphere. The accommodations are spacious, many with large balconies. The sporting facilities offered by the hotel - an indoor swimming pool as well as indoor and outdoor tennis courts - are in keeping with and complement the resort setting. The hotel opens on to grazing grounds, prohibited from development by the town. Across this park like pasture guests can absorb some of the region's most spectacular mountain vistas. Stay here, enjoy the luxury of the facilities, be pampered by the service, and pretend that you are, perhaps, one of the royalty for whom Mr Ruchti built the hotel.

*HOTEL VICTORIA JUNGFRAU*
*Director: Emanuel Berger*
*Hoheweg 41*
*CH-3800 Interlaken, Switzerland*
*tel: (036) 21 21 71  fax: (036) 22 26 71*
*228 Rooms: Sfr 280-420*
*Open: mid-Dec to mid-Nov*
*Credit cards: All major*
*U.S. Rep: Leading Hotels of the World*
*Rep tel: 800-223-6800*
*Located 175 km S of Zurich*

The Royal Hotel Bellevue enjoys a most special position in the middle of the Bernese Oberland, between Gstaad and Interlaken - easily reached in three hours by direct train from the Zurich airport. Kandersteg offers a hikers' paradise through protected valleys to woods, mountain-lakes and glaciers. The rear of the Royal Bellevue affords splendid views across gorgeous meadows to the soaring mountain peaks. The wide lawns of the hotel in summer are a velvet carpet of grass. In the garden is an outdoor pool; inside is another pool, sauna and solarium. The Royal Bellevue, although recently constructed, reflects an olde-worlde elegance with cavernous fireplaces, comfy leather sofas, 18th-century tapestries on the walls and a scattering of antiques to accentuate the traditional ambiance. The dining room is especially elegant: tables set with crisp white tablecloths, upholstered armchairs and giant chandeliers. (Appropriate dress is requested for dinner.) The bedrooms are elaborately decorated - some of the furnishings a bit too ornate for my taste - but very luxurious. In addition to the swimming pools, the hotel has its own riding stables, plus motor and sail boats (on nearby Lake Thun). Like so many of the excellent inns within Switzerland, the gracious owner, Albert Rikli, is the third generation in the hotel profession.

*ROYAL HOTEL BELLEVUE*
*Hotelier: Familie A. Rikli*
*CH-3718 Kandersteg, Switzerland*
*tel: (033) 75 12 12   fax: (033) 75 13 33*
*35 Rooms: Sfr 235-500*
*Open: Dec to Apr & Jun to Oct*
*Credit cards: All major*
*U.S. Rep: Leading Hotels of the World*
*Rep tel: 800-223-6800*
*Outdoor & indoor pools*
*Located 200 km S of Zurich*

Almost considered a landmark of Switzerland, the Kleine Scheidegg Hotel sits on a barren, windswept landscape that challenges all but the giant Eiger. It is recognized by many for its part in the staging of the adventure movie "The Eiger Sanction". The public rooms are attractive with a turn-of-the-century mountain hotel ambiance. I could not see any of the guest rooms since at the time of our visit the rooms were all reserved. When I attempted to question the receptionist about the accommodations and their decor, I was told in a very matter-of-fact manner, "Of course they are lovely, if the rooms were not nice why else would the hotel always be full and people return year after year?" If not an informative description, it does seem a logical answer. The town of Kleine Scheidegg consists of just a few sparsely scattered buildings serving as the junction for trains from Grindelwald and Lauterbrunnen bound for the Jungfraujoch. But even though quite isolated, in summer Kleine Scheidegg is bustling with activity. Many hikers can be seen having a snack before heading off on their adventures and tourists bask in the sun while waiting for their train up to the Jungfrau.

*KLEINE SCHEIDEGG HOTEL*
*Hotelier: Frau Heidi von Almen*
*CH-3801 Kleine Scheidegg*
*Switzerland*
*tel: (036) 55 12 12  fax: (036) 55 12 94*
*92 Rooms: Sfr 220-280 (with 2 meals)*
*Open: Dec to Apr & Jun to Oct*
*Credit cards: VS, MC, DC*
*Convenient location for Jungfrau trip*
*Located 210 km S of Zurich*

It had been 12 years since I had visited the Chesa Grischuna, but the memories of that visit lingered with such vivid pleasure that I knew if the hotel still existed I would want to include it in this guide.  The season was different, winter's cozy blanket of snow having turned with spring into clusters of brightly colored flowers, but the interior was as I remembered - romantic and cozy.   We were first here on a ski holiday, and the warmth of the Chesa Grischuna was one of the few temptations to succeed in getting us off the slope.   Mellow, weathered paneling enriches most of the public rooms, while antique furnishings and accents of copper pieces and artistic flower arrangements blend beautifully.  Without the benefit of antiques, the bedrooms achieve the country feeling with the use of charming provincial wallpapers and matching fabrics, copies of traditional Swiss furniture, exposed beams and gently sloping floors.   Some of the bedrooms are a bit cozy and small, but all nicely done, and if you are on a budget you might want to consider a room without bath.   The dining room is exceptional in cuisine, service and "country formal" atmosphere.   The personality of the staff matches the character and charm of the inn.

*HOTEL CHESA GRISCHUNA*
*Hotelier: Hans & Doris Guler*
*CH-7250 Klosters, Switzerland*
*tel: (083) 4 22 22*
*fax: (081) 69 22 25 (after May 1990)*
*26 Rooms: Sfr 190-310 (includes 2 meals)*
*Open: All year*
*Credit cards: All major*
*U.S. Rep: Romantik Hotels*
*Rep tel: 800-826-0015*
*Cozy chalet-style inn*
*Located 150 km E of Zurich*

The Hotel du Lac Seehof is located on Lake Lucerne at Kussnacht. Many steamers that ply the lake stop here, and as the hotel is ideally situated directly on the waterfront where the boats dock, it serves as a popular luncheon spot. The town of Kussnacht is rather noisy and bustling with tourists, but you have a feeling of tranquillity in the oasis of the hotel's terrace restaurant. (The garden restaurant is a very popular attraction for tourists who have taken the boat for a day's adventure from Lucerne.) The Hotel du Lac Seehof has been in the Trutmann family for five generations and is now managed by Albert Trutmann and his attractive wife, Joan. Albert Trutmann lived in the United States for a number of years, speaks perfect English and understands American tastes. Downstairs, the dining room to the left of the front hall is delightfully decorated with antiques. It has a certain elegance, but is not pretentious. Mr Trutmann showed me the bedrooms which have been redecorated, 8 rooms have private bathrooms and 9 have bathrooms down the hall.

*HOTEL DU LAC SEEHOF*
*Hotelier: Albert & Joan Trutmann*
*CH-6403 Kussnacht am Rigi*
*Switzerland*
*tel: (041) 81 10 12  fax: (041) 81 56 96*
*17 Rooms: Sfr 66-130*
*Credit cards: All major*
*Open: All year*
*Lakeside setting - next to pier*
*Located 13 km NE of Lucerne*

Meandering through the serenely beautiful Emmental Valley when researching the first edition of our Swiss guide, I had happened upon the Hotel Hirschen. I remember being captivated by the small inn's wonderfully cozy facade of many little shuttered windows sheltered by a deeply overhanging roof - a typical Emmental chalet. But on my first visit I thought the guest rooms needed a "touch up". Happily, the hotel has been refurbished and now, outside and inside, it is quite delightful. There are several dining rooms, extremely popular, especially on Sundays when the rooms are bustling with the warmth of families sharing the noonday meal. And the food is excellent: the kitchen has earned many honors, including Officier Maitre Chaine des Rotisseur and Commandeur des Cordons Bleus de France. To accompany your meal you can choose from 24,000 bottles of wine stored in a 15th-century wine cellar. There are only a few guest rooms. These are simply decorated, but pleasant, with light wooden built-in furniture, good reading lights and modern bathrooms. The town of Langnau is one of the most charming in the Emmental Valley.

*HOTEL HIRSCHEN*
*Hotelier: Familie Birkhauser*
*Dorfstrasse 17*
*CH-3550 Langnau im Emmental*
*Switzerland*
*tel: (035) 215 17  fax: (035) 256 23*
*18 Rooms: Sfr 80-130*
*Open: Feb to Dec*
*Credit cards: All major*
*Cozy Emmental-style chalet*
*Located 110 km W of Zurich*

As you drive through the village of Lenzerheide you are surrounded by the commercialism of a major ski resort - too modern, too new.  But take the small road leading up the hill and suddenly you are in a high mountain hamlet, surrounded by some of the most spectacular vistas in all of Switzerland: the softness of mountain meadows enhance the backdrop of mighty mountain peaks.  Nothing mars the landscape dotted by only by a few weathered farmhouses.  You have found your hotel, the Guarda Val.  At first glance one would never guess that a deluxe hotel is nestled into this tiny village, but closer inspection reveals a gourmet restaurant in one building, a Swiss regional restaurant in another and guest rooms cleverly incorporated into a selection of smaller farmhouses.  In winter the fields are blanketed with snow - a mecca for the skier.  In summer the meadows are sprinkled with wild flowers and laced with paths - a delight for the hiker.  The guest rooms vary.  Some are decorated with modern wallpapers and bright colors.  My favorite rooms are those more traditional in decor, with soft muted colors.  But, whatever your taste, I cannot imagine a more idyllic setting for a luxury resort.  The Hotel Guarda Val is a member of the prestigious *Relais & Chateaux* group.

*HOTEL GUARDA VAL*
*Hotelier: Heinz & Beatrice Wehrle*
*CH-7078 Lenzerheide, Switzerland*
*tel: (081) 34 22 14  fax: (081) 34 46 45*
*36 Rooms: Sfr 180-400*
*Open: Jun to Oct & Dec to mid-Apr*
*Tennis, hiking, sauna, skiing*
*Hotel incorporated into small village*
*Located 150 km SW of Zurich*

On a gloriously sunny day I rode the tram to the top of the hillside to further investigate the Hotel Chateau Gutsch.  Settling on the hotel's terrace, I was captivated by the panorama of Lucerne stretching before me: an incredibly lovely bird's-eye view of the city nestling next to the blue lake.  My impression of the hotel on an earlier visit had been that it was a bit too dramatic and ornately decorated to include in a book of country inns - however, the day and the view erased any previous reservations.  Turrets, balconies and terraces dress the Chateau Gutsch in almost a fairy tale atmosphere.  When travelling with children the hotel's large swimming pool and wooded grounds would prove an added bonus and a welcome respite from sightseeing and long drives.  The dining room enjoys a country ambiance with wooden tables and chairs, large wine casks and an enormous fireplace, and the food is excellent.  If you prefer a hotel a bit out of the bustle of the center of Lucerne, you can't go wrong with the Hotel Chateau Gutsch.

*HOTEL CHATEAU GUTSCH*
*Manager: Mr. A. Panayiopou*
*Kanonenstrasse*
*CH-6003 Lucerne, Switzerland*
*tel: (041) 22 02 72  fax: (041) 22 02 52*
*40 Rooms: Sfr 247-278*
*Open: All year*
*Credit cards: All major*
*U.S. Rep: Utell International*
*Rep tel: 800-223-9868*
*Gorgeous lake views*
*Located on hill overlooking Lucerne*

The Wilden Mann is unique - an oasis of charm and hospitality located in the heart of the medieval city of Lucerne.   The Wilden Mann has been in the Furler family for many years and their love and caring is very evident.   The hotel has a "genuine" feel of quality: lovely antiques are used everywhere, not only in the lobby and lounges, but also scattered artistically throughout the hotel.   There are three dining rooms, each delightful in its own way.   The "Liedertafel" is a French-style restaurant with pink tablecloths, candlelight, and, in cold weather, a cozy fire. This dining room has a special feature: on one of the walls there are framed three scenes depicting the Wilden Mann as it has progressed from its origins in 1517. The most unusual scene is when the hotel was originally built - at that time a river ran in front of the hotel, complete with a drawbridge to the entrance.   Upstairs there is another dining area - an outdoor garden terrace where tables are set for dining on warm summer days.   But my favorite place to dine is the "Burgerstube", a cozy, charming, very Swiss country-style dining room with an ambiance of informality and warmth.   Around the tables are wonderful wooden chairs - many of them genuine antiques.   The room's atmosphere is accentuated with wrought iron artifacts and colorful crests bordering the wall.   Should you want to have a drink before your meal, there is an exceptionally cozy bar on the second floor.

Since the Wilden Mann is such an old building the bedrooms vary considerably.   If you are travelling with friends you might each have a room entirely different in size and style of decor even through the price is similar.   However, this is one of the charms of the hotel; it is not a large commercial operation where everything has a stamp of "plastic" sameness.   Instead, each bedroom varies as it would if you were a guest in a friend's home.   Many are decorated in coordinating colors with attractive bedspreads matching the wall paper and draperies.   All of the rooms I saw were delightful.   Even the singles have charm.   On one of my research trips I fell in love with my room, quite small but appealingly furnished with a single bed, dresser and desk - a perfect oasis to sit writing hotel descriptions while overlooking the weathered, red-tiled rooftops of Lucerne. It is no wonder that each detail of decor throughout the hotel is so perfect - Mrs Furler personally supervises the decorating down to the selection of the fabrics used and the placement of the antiques. It is her caring touch which helps to make the Wilden Mann so warm and home-like. I have never met Mrs Furler, but her husband is most charming and personally oversees the operation of the hotel. The inn has been in the same family since the 19th century and the Furlers carry on the tradition that "every guest be pampered in this house."

On their first visit to Lucerne, many tourist opt for one of the hotels along the lake. However, my choice is to be in the heart of historical old Lucerne where one is immersed in the romance of days gone by. Lucerne is such a convenient, "walkable" city, that no matter where you stay, all the sights are available by foot. And, the Wilden Mann it is just a pleasant walk to the lake.

*WILDEN MANN HOTEL*
*Hotelier: Fritz Furler*
*Manager: Mrs Susi Rick*
*Bahnhofstrasse 30*
*CH-6003 Lucerne, Switzerland*
*tel: (041) 23 16 66  fax: (041) 23 16 29*
*50 Rooms: Sfr 252-282*
*Open: All year*
*Credit cards: All major*
*U.S. Rep: Romantik Hotels*
*Rep tel: 800-826-0015*
*Charming small inn*
*Located in the heart of old Lucerne*

Lucerne is an expensive city, so we decided to suggest one less costly hotel for those who need to watch their budget. The atmospheric Hotel Schlussel (although we want to stress this is a modest inn) offers a very good value. A large golden key and a Swiss flag hang from the flower-adorned facade to welcome guests. Located off a small side street on a tiny historical square, the Hotel Schlussel faces an old church and enjoys a relatively quiet corner in this bustling city. The hotel is a pretty medieval house which has been converted into a refreshing little city hotel. The Schlussel's historic beer-stube restaurant has beamed ceilings, old leaded glass windows, and is often frequented by locals for an afternoon drink. There are also cozy nooks where guests enjoy traditional home-cooked meals. Freshly painted white hallways lead to the newly renovated bedrooms, almost all of which have private bath or shower. The airy rooms are furnished with light-colored, modern furniture and tasteful fabrics with a greenery motif. Frau Gressner tends to all aspects of the hotel with care and provides her guests with a warm welcome. Offering only 11 rooms, the Schlussel is an intimate little hotel, and reservations should be made well in advance in order to enjoy a stay here.

*HOTEL SCHLUSSEL*
*Owner: Frau M.M. Gressner*
*Franziskanerplatz 12*
*CH-6000 Lucerne*
*Switzerland*
*tel: (041) 23 10 61*
*11 Rooms - Double to Sfr 90*
*Open: All year*
*Credit cards: None accepted*
*Located in the historic old part of the city*

The medieval section of Lugano is a marvelous maze of twisting alleys, stairways and pedestrian streets, and a delightful confusion of little squares, restaurants, and boutiques.   The Ticino is appropriately located right at the "heart" of the old city, on one of its most charming little squares.   Although the hotel is in an area closed to traffic, if you have luggage you can drive in front of the hotel to unload your suitcases before parking your car.   On the ground floor of the hotel you will discover a tiny lobby and an intimate dining room serving fabulous meals which are as popular with the locals as with the tourists.   There is a wonderful inner courtyard (reflecting the hotel's past history as a convent) which adds an appealing garden atmosphere to the hotel.   The bedrooms and lounge areas are found on the upper floors.   Each level is bright with flowers and greenery and graced with some lovely paintings and handsome antiques.   The Hotel Ticino is a wonderful old Tessin house, owned and operated by the Buchmann family who effectively practice their motto "to serve is our duty - to serve well our pleasure".

*HOTEL TICINO*
*Hotelier: Claire & Samuel Buchmann*
*Piazza Cioccaro 1*
*CH-6901 Lugano, Switzerland*
*tel: (091) 22 77 72  fax: (091) 23 62 78*
*23 Rooms: Sfr 253-308*
*Open: Feb to Dec*
*Credit cards: All major*
*U.S. Rep: Romantik Hotels*
*Rep tel: 800-826-0015*
*Located in the heart of old Lugano*

The Villa Principe Leopoldo is located in the hills to the southwest of Lugano - about a 10-minute drive away by complimentary transportation.   The hotel is very impressive from the first encounter - a stately, two-story, ocher-colored building, softened by vines which lace the front and enhanced by a heavy red-tiled roof accented by many small chimneys of all shapes and sizes.   This isn't just any villa - the Villa Principe Leopoldo was, as the name implies, at one time the residence of princes.   For those who love opulence - this is the hotel for you.   The air of sophistication is set as you enter the long reception hall with its creamy-white marble floors, stately marble columns and potted palms.   The living room, bar, and dining room maintain the same air of elegance with abundant use of rich fabrics and modern decor.   My favorite rooms are the bedrooms - each a suite with a spacious sleeping area divided by tie-back draperies from the sitting area which has a sofa, desk and chairs.   A hint at the clientele of this fancy hotel is that each room not only has the bedside phone, but also a portable phone so that the guests can keep in touch at all times with important business matters at home.   If one should tire of just sipping drinks on the terrace overlooking the lake, the Villa Principe Leopoldo offers a wealth of facilities: swimming pool, tennis, sauna, etc.

*VILLA PRINCIPE LEOPOLDO*
*Manager: C. Fattore*
*Via Montalbano 5*
*CH-6900 Lugano, Switzerland*
*tel: (091) 55 85 55  fax: (091) 54 25 38*
*24 suites: Sfr 350-450*
*Credit cards: All major*
*Pool, tennis, sauna, gymnasium, solarium*
*Located 10 minutes SW of Lugano*

Romantically perched in the hills overlooking Lake Lugano is the beautiful Villa Margherita.   The fragrance of roses blends with the singing of birds as you enter this oasis of tranquillity.   Although you are in Switzerland, the mood is definitely Italian, with the heavily tiled roof and green shutters setting off the pastel colored villa.   Surrounding the original villa are a cluster of smaller villas beautifully designed within the gardens: some of these are very old, some are of new construction, but all are harmonious.   A large outdoor pool nestles on one of the villa's many scenic terraces while a smaller pool snuggles into the gardens by one of the little villas.   An indoor salt-water pool completes the scene.   Although a superb, sophisticated elegance pervades the mood of this deluxe hotel, owned and personally managed by the gracious Herzog family, the ambiance is one of warmth and geniality.   The Herzog family's caring is felt in every detail from the perfection of the gardens to the kitchen (the food is sensational).   So if you would prefer to be away from the hustle of Lugano and savor the beauty of Lake Lugano from isolated splendor, I highly recommend the Villa Margherita.   The hotel belongs to the prestigious *Relais & Chateaux* hotel group.

*VILLA MARGHERITA*
*Hotelier: Familie Herzog*
*CH-6935 Bosco-Luganese*
*Switzerland*
*tel: (091) 59 14 31  fax: (091) 50 61 49*
*37 Rooms: Sfr 210-280*
*Open: Apr 1 to Oct 24*
*Credit cards: All major*
*Overlooking the lake*
*2 outdoor pools, 1 indoor pool*
*Located 7 km NW of Lugano*

The Elvezia al Lago is an attractive small hotel peacefully located along the lakeside footpath joining the towns of Castagnola and Gandria. There are seven guest rooms, each with its own bathroom and a balcony overlooking the lake. There is a cozy small restaurant on the first floor of the hotel, but the favorite place to eat is the terrace restaurant on the edge of the water. The Elvezia al Lago is pretty, with a white facade cheerfully enhanced by blue and white awnings - a color scheme repeated in the blue striped awning over the waterside terrace and the blue checked tablecloths. Because the hotel is small, Mr Lucke cannot accept reservations for less than five days, but if you call him upon your arrival in Switzerland, he will be delighted to arrange a room for a shorter stay if space is available. The Elvezia al Lago is a bit tricky to find. If you are driving from Lugano, head east toward Castagnola. Just beyond the museum "Villa Favorita", take Via Cortivo, a small road which ends in a parking area called San Domenico. Call from the phone booth in the parking area - Mr Lucke will send a boat to pick you up at the adjacent dock. (If you prefer to walk, you can take the footpath from the parking area along the "Sentiero di Gandria" continuing east along the lake until you arrive at the hotel - about a 7 minute walk.) If you do not have a car, you can take the ferry from Lugano to the hotel (boat stop is "Grotto Elvezia").

*ELVEZIA AL LAGO*
*Hotelier: Herbert & Doris Lucke*
*Santiero di Gandria, 21*
*CH-6976 Lugano-Castagnola, Switzerland*
*tel: (091) 51 44 51*
*7 Rooms: Sfr 130*
*Open: Apr to end of October*
*Credit cards: All major*
*Located 1.2 km E of Lugano*

The Carina is situated directly on the road facing Lake Lugano in the picturesque small village of Morcote, only about a 15-minute drive south of Lugano.  Across the street from the hotel is an outdoor cafe suspended on stilts out over the lake. Flowers and a brightly striped awning add even further fun to this dining haven. An inside dining room has a wooden beamed ceiling, white walls accented by green plants, and a few well placed antiques and oriental rugs - a very inviting room decorated with style and good taste.   The hotel is built into the hillside and there are a series of stories as the rooms climb the hill.   The bedrooms in front can be a bit noisy with the traffic on the street below, but they are still my favorites. Quieter rooms are found in the back, many of which look out onto the small pool snuggled in the upper terrace above the hotel.   If you really want to splurge, room 45 is very special - a large bright corner room with two balconies, one looking out over the tiled rooftops to the lake and the other overlooking the pool with a vista to the church.

The Hotel Carina has another real advantage: the owners, Heidi and Horst Echsle who both speak English perfectly.   Heidi is usually at the reception desk.   Her sincere warmth and friendliness, combined with a twinkling sense of humor, make each guest feel immediately "at home".   This is another hotel at which the owners are very involved with the management and the hotel shows their love and caring. As I walked through the hotel it looked as if a meticulous housewife had just been through before me arranging lovely bouquets of flowers, adjusting each painting, fluffing each pillow.   Each detail showed lovely taste and concern with the comfort of the guest.   Horst Echsle oversees the kitchen and the food is fabulous.

So try to plan your trip to linger in Morcote.   Perhaps for the first few days just sleep late and enjoy the view from your room before moving out to the terrace for lunch.   Then perhaps venture a little further to visit the lovely Parco Scherrer, a splendid garden, located a five-minute walk from the hotel. Then, completely refreshed, venture further to explore the tiny villages along the lake. Just a few steps from the hotel the ferry boats pull into the dock, so climb on board to explore the small villages tucked into tiny coves around the lake. What fun to float from one charming town to another, getting off to sample the food from little waterfront cafes. What a perfect holiday.

If you want to make your base in Morcote while in Switzerland's beautiful southern lake district, the Hotel Carina makes a convenient possibility. You do not need a car: the boat can whisk you to Lugano for a day of shopping; another boat will take you to Villa Favorita (one of Europe's finest small museums) located in a wonderful old villa along the lake; a boat and train combination can take you to visit Ascona, a charming little town on Lake Maggiore.

*HOTEL CARINA*
*Hotelier: Heidi & Horst Echsle*
*CH-6922 Lugano-Morcote*
*Switzerland*
*tel: (091) 69 11 31  fax: (091) 69 19 29*
*19 Rooms: Sfr 135-228*
*Open: Mar to Nov*
*Credit cards: All major*
*Overlooking Lake Lugano*
*Pool tucked into upper terrace*
*Located 6 km S of Lugano*

My anticipation was high as we drove up to Le Vieux Manoir au Lac as I had already fallen in love with the image projected by the brochure. I was not disappointed. The hotel is a wonderful combination of weathered wood, stucco, little gables, high pitched roofs, overhanging eaves and whimsical chimneys. A warm sunny day completed what seemed a perfect welcome. Our room, which looked out over the expanse of lawn and the peaceful lake, was small but nicely decorated with a provincial print that covered the walls and ceiling, and extended into the dressing area and bathroom. All the other bedrooms seemed delightful as I peeked over the maids' shoulders while they were making them up the next morning - room 6 had a large canopy bed and room 24 a lake view. That night we ate a la carte - a delicious meal of fresh fish and green salad. There were several choices for complete dinners though they seemed quite expensive. The atmosphere of the dining room was romantic, with lovely table settings and fresh flowers. A perfect end to a perfect day.

*LE VIEUX MANOIR AU LAC*
*Hotelier: Erich Thomas*
*CH-3280 Murten-Meyriez, Switzerland*
*tel: (037) 71 12 83   fax: (037) 71 31 88*
*23 Rooms: Sfr 170-280; 2 tower suites: Sfr 360*
*Open: mid-Feb to Dec*
*Credit cards: VS, DC*
*Lovely lake setting*
*Located 120 km NE of Geneva*

The Hotel Chasa Chalavaina, although quite a simple little inn, has a remarkably sophisticated charm.   Fresh white walls and an open, uncluttered decor give the hotel a crisp, airy atmosphere.   The dining room is decorated with wonderful wooden country-style furniture and has a beautiful antique ceramic stove - in bygone days the only source of heat.   I struggled to explain to the owner, Mr Jon Fasser, who unfortunately for me did not speak English, that I would like permission to take photos and to see some bedrooms. We were not communicating too well when I was approached by a charming Swiss lady, obviously a guest at the hotel, who had been listening to the conversation and offered to assist.   She delayed her departure for a day's excursion to take me under her wing and show me the entire hotel.   First we saw her room, delightful with country-style decor and a beautiful balcony overlooking the valley.   My new-found friend and I then peeked into every nook and cranny (luckily most of the guests were already out for the day), including the kitchen, dining rooms and bar.   The guest rooms I saw were extremely pleasant - bright and airy with nice views from the windows. After the "tour", my friend rejoined her husband whom she had deposited at the hotel's arched entrance, said good bye and was on her way.

*HOTEL CHASA CHALAVAINA*
*Hotelier: Jon Fasser*
*CH-7537 Mustair, Switzerland*
*tel: (082) 8 54 68*
*16 Rooms: Sfr 80-120*
*Open: All year*
*Credit cards: None*
*Delightful small inn*
*Located 250 km E of Zurich*

The Hotel Du Clos de Sadex is located about 26 kilometers from Geneva on the north shore of Lake Geneva. The hotel's address is written as Nyon, but it is actually on the main, lakeside road, just a short distance east of the town. Surrounded by its own quiet expanse of gardens, once an elegant patrician estate, the home is now converted into a hotel. Some of the bedrooms are in the main villa, while the others are located in a very lovely annex next door. The bedrooms vary in size and decor, and although some have been recently refurbished, those I saw on my most recent inspection still needed sprucing up. However, there is a casual, lovable charm to this small hotel. The staff is extremely hospitable and cordial, and the downstairs public rooms are very cozy and charming. Oriental rugs enrich wooden parquet floors and antiques are handsomely displayed throughout. The greatest asset of this small hotel is the setting: the gardens behind the hotel stretch out to the lake and green lawns, flowers, and shade trees create a tranquil scene. The Hotel du Clos de Sadex is so small that you will feel like a guest in a private home.

*HOTEL DU CLOS DE SADEX*
*Hotelier: L. de Tscharner*
*CH-1260 Nyon*
*Switzerland*
*tel: (022) 61 28 31*
*18 Rooms: Sfr 166-234*
*Open: Mar to Jan*
*Credit cards: All major*
*Lake setting*
*Located 26 km E of Geneva*

The Rote Rose is my idea of THE PERFECT INN - it has everything: an owner, Christa Schafer, who is one of the finest hostesses I have ever had the pleasure to meet - a truly beautiful person with a special quality of sincere warmth and hospitality; an idyllic setting on the knoll of a hill with a splendid view; a sensational position in the heart of a medieval village; the delightful ambiance of a beautifully restored historic building; a romantic history; an interior filled with antiques; and one of Switzerland's finest restaurants next door.   And, if this is not enough to win your heart, the walls are filled with the paintings of the renowned rose artist, Lotte Gunthart, Christa's mother.   Lotte Gunthart's contribution to the world of roses has been so significant that an especially beautiful red rose is named for her.

Regensberg is very difficult to find on any but the most detailed map.   However, it is just a few minutes from Dielsdorf which is much easier to locate.   Actually, Regensberg is almost a suburb of Zurich - being near the airport or about a 25-minute drive northwest of the city.   Although near Zurich geographically, it is worlds away in mood.

*Regensberg*

Regensberg is a tiny village founded by the Baron Lutold V in 1245. I don't know who Lutold was, but he certainly knew a beautiful location when he found it: the town is so perfectly situated that there is a 360-degree view. You can spot Regensberg as you leave Dielsdorf - it is perched on a nearby hilltop with a fairy tale view out over the vineyards all the way to Zurich. On a clear day magnificent mountains frame the horizon.

The Rote Rose has no restaurant within the building, but right next door is the Gasthaus Krone, an excellent restaurant. It is closed from lunch time on Sunday until dinner on Tuesday. (If you arrive on Sunday or Monday, you can enjoy a delightful meal in a small hotel, the Hotel Loewen, owned by the Schafer family, just a few kilometers away in Dielsdorf.) Since there is no restaurant at the Rote Rose, breakfast is served next door at the Gasthaus Krone or brought to your room.

As you can surmise from the above write up, the Rote Rose is one of our favorite places to recommend, but the problem has been that with only 2 rooms, it was very difficult to secure space. Happily, we can now report that fewer travellers will be disappointed because there are more accommodations: 3 suites and 2 rooms are now available. However, the Rote Rose has so many repeat guests, it is still very important to call well in advance for your reservation.

*ROTE ROSE*
*Hotelier: Christa Schafer*
*CH-8158 Regensberg (Dielsdorf), Switzerland*
*tel: (01) 853 1013   or   (01) 853 0080*
*2 Rooms: $150;   3 Suites: $200 (US dollars)*
*Credit cards: None accepted*
*Exquisite tiny hotel in a medieval village*
*Located 20 minutes from the Zurich airport*

The Waldhotel Fletschhorn is located on a little branch of the valley leading to the more famous resort of Zermatt, but Zermatt is located on the valley floor encircled by the mountains while Saas-Fee is up in the mountains. When you leave the Rhone Valley, heading for Zermatt, the road splits. You take the left branch which continues through the valley then climbs up the mountain ending in a huge, rather ugly concrete parking lot in Saas-Fee. But do not be discouraged. The town itself is most picturesque. After parking, go to the tourist office next to Parking Lot 1, push the indicated button and you will be automatically connected with the Waldhotel Fletschhorn. Someone will come in about ten minutes to pick you up in a little electric cart which takes you through the village, out into an open field, enters a dense forest, and then, like magic, comes to a wonderful open meadow perched high above the valley. Here, in isolated splendor, is the Waldhotel Fletschhorn. Although the hotel appears to be new, it actually dates back to the 18th century. Outside there is a large terrace where guests can soak up the sun - and the view. This terrace is the gathering place in summer for hikers to enjoy a cold drink and share their day's adventures. Inside, there is a country ambiance with a nice selection of antiques setting an informal, friendly mood.

When I visited the Waldhotel Fletschhorn all the rooms were occupied, but I did manage to see many of them while guests were at dinner. Each varies in size and decor. Rooms are very pleasant, some with enormous bathrooms and view balconies. My favorite was room 15, all alone on a lower level below the parking lot. This room has a fairy tale view of the valley plus a cozy decor.

One of the hotel's best features has been saved for last. Here in the middle of nowhere is a woman gourmet cook proclaimed to be the best in Switzerland. She is Irma Dutsch, the owner's wife. Irma is not only an incredible cook, but she also sparkles with personality and makes her guests feel like personal friends whom she is pleased to welcome into her home. When I asked her more details on her reputation as a gourmet chef, she showed me photographs of some of her culinary creations being used in television programs, and clippings from various magazines around the world. At dinner Irma promised to prepare a selection of her delicacies for us. I could not believe my eyes at what appeared. Seven courses arrived - each more beautifully displayed than the previous one. Exotic, delicious entrees such as quail's egg souffle with lobster sauce. During one course I was admiring the beautiful flower design on my plate, only to realize on closer inspection that actually I was eating off two plates. The lower plate was white china with an artistic arrangement of fresh wild flowers. On top was pressed a clear crystal plate through which the flowers below showed in an exquisite design. I should mention that this dinner was "special" for us, although a la carte meals can be ordered. However, as I looked about me the "standard" dinners looked absolutely delicious and beautifully prepared. My final thought as we reluctantly left the Waldhotel Fletschhorn was that thank goodness there were so many beautiful walking trails leading off from the hotel - with Irma Dutsch's gourmet cooking, walking would be a prerequisite for survival. This is a restful place - plan to stay three days or more.

*WALDHOTEL FLETSCHHORN*
*Hotelier: Hansjorg & Irma Dutsch*
*CH-3906 Saas-Fee, Switzerland*
*tel: (028) 57 21 31  fax: (028) 57 21 87*
*10 Rooms: Sfr 300 (with 2 meals)*
*Open: Christmas to Easter & Jun to Oct*
*Credit Cards: All major*
*Wonderful mountain setting*
*Exceptional gourmet meals*
*Located 200 km SE of Geneva*

The Hotel Kreuz, a few blocks off the main highway, does not look too promising from the outside. It is a stately old manor home behind which is a rather uninteresting motel section. However, what a surprise inside. Although a large hotel, it is decorated with great charm. The hotel has been in the same family since 1489 and family antiques are used throughout - old chests, wonderful clocks, cradles, armories, paintings, antique tables, beautiful old chairs, and other heirlooms highlight the tasteful decor in all the public rooms. Although some of the guest rooms are uninterestingly situated in a motel-like annex, others are outstanding. I was shown an old wooden Swiss chalet located next to the main hotel. Rooms 1 and 2 in this little cottage are lovingly restored and decorated in simple country style, very appropriate for a house dating back 400 years. This little wooden chalet is called the "colored house" because it used to be painted red, which signified that this was the home of the magistrate - the most important man in town. In the rear of the main residence is an old mill which has also been converted into hotel rooms. Here, suite 73, is one of the most beautifully decorated rooms I had seen in Switzerland - splurge ask for this divine suite. As an added bonus, the hotel has its own small garden area on the lake. *Note: Just as we were going to press we received a letter from the Hotel Kreuz that the hotel has been completely rebuilt, but maintains the same delightful olde worlde ambiance.*

*HOTEL KREUZ*
*Manager: Mr. Sprokkerees*
*CH-6072 Sachseln, Switzerland*
*tel: (041) 66 14 66  fax: (041) 66 81 88*
*60 Rooms: Sfr 135-156*
*Open: All year*
*Credit Cards: All major*
*Located 80 km S of Zurich*

The Chasa Capol is a unique hotel located on the main street of the small town of Santa Maria in the beautiful Mustair Valley. The colorful background of the inn given to me by the owner stated: "The foundation of Chasa Capol dates back to the 8th century. Over the centuries, it was the property of the noble family De Capol as well as the valley governor's residence. The Capol's genealogical tree has been traced back to the Venetian, Marco Polo." The hotel's history piqued my imagination, and it alone would have merited a visit to this beautiful remote valley. I loved the Chasa Capol from the moment I walked into the small lobby and was warmly welcomed. The owners, Mr and Mrs Ernst Schweizer, speak no English, but their smile of welcome is an international language. Fortunately for the guests, a most delightful young lady, Karin Hansen, speaks English fluently. She has been with the hotel for many years and can answer your questions, offer sightseeing suggestions, or even arrange a chauffeur-driven car, should you so desire. I became friends with Karin on my first visit and am pleased to find she is still with the Schweizers - and as gracious as ever.

The bedrooms have names which represent famous guests. Our room, "Guerg Jenatsch", overlooked the back garden. It has twin beds joined by a wooden headboard painted green with reading lamps on either side. On the beds are the ever-present fluffy down comforters covered with a delightful red and green provincial print fabric plus a small writing table with chair and lamp. Rag rugs on the floor and cheerful green print draperies on the window complete the scene.

The dining room is charming, with light antique wood furniture, flowers everywhere and wonderful food. Mrs Schweizer is an accomplished chef who adds her talents in personally supervising the kitchen. To complement the meal the Chasa Capol has its own vineyards and serves an excellent Gewurztraminer house wine. The hotel even has its own casks of wine stored in the cellar. The hotel has many other special features including a wonderful little theater, a small museum and a small pool in the rear garden (a welcome addition on a warm summer day, especially if travelling with children).

The Schweizers are lovingly restoring this wonderful historical building. The hotel almost has a museum quality, with a small chapel in the basement with precious icons, a little theater in the attic where special concerts are still given, plus artifacts throughout such as antique costumes and old sleds. Staying at the Chasa Capol is truly like stepping back in time to enjoy the ambiance of yesterday with the amenities of today.

Note: The Schweizers have opened a small "bed and breakfast" across the street in an old house called "Villetta Capolina" for those on a budget. Although the rooms do not have private bathrooms, they are decorated in a romantic style and cost only Sfr 55 per person. There is also an apartment available which has a kitchenette.

*THEATER-HOTEL CHASA CAPOL*
*Hotelier: Mr & Mrs Ernest Schweizer*
*Receptionist: Karin Hanser*
*CH-7536 Santa Maria, Switzerland*
*tel: (082) 8 57 28*
*20 Rooms: Sfr 120-200*
*Open: All year*
*Credit Cards: None*
*Inn dating from the 8th century*
*Small museum, family chapel*
*In-house theater, wine cellar*
*Small swimming pool in garden*
*Located 230 km E of Zurich*

The Domaine de Chateauvieux is located just a 20-minute drive from the Geneva airport, a convenient hotel choice for a first night in Switzerland.   It is difficult to comprehend that you are only a few miles west of a large city as you approach this 15th-century stone manor.   On the knoll of a hill laced with fields of vineyards, it seems miles from a cosmopolitan center.   In the courtyard is an old wine press and in the summer an abundance of bright flowers. Inside the Domaine de Chateauvieux there is a lovely dining room with a tasteful array of antiques gracefully intermingled with new furnishings to give a feeling of coziness and warmth.   When I first visited there were only 12 guest rooms, each pleasantly decorated and with views of the vineyards.   Recently Mr and Mrs Gnazzo, who own other hotels in Geneva, purchased the hotel and have added 6 more rooms. For those who prefer country living to the big cities the Domaine de Chateauvieux would be a very good alternative to staying in Geneva.   You could have the best of two worlds by staying in the country with only a short drive into Geneva for sightseeing.

*AUBERGE DE CHATEAUVIEUX*
*Hotelier: Mr and Mrs Gnazzo*
*Peney-Dessus*
*CH-1242 Satigny, Switzerland*
*tel: (022) 753 15 11*
*18 Rooms: Sfr 140-180*
*Open: All year*
*Credit Cards: All major*
*15th-century country manor*
*Located few km W of Geneva*

The Rheinhotel Fischerzunft is beautifully situated along the banks of the Rhine. The ferry leaves only a few steps from the hotel - making it a most convenient choice if you want to explore the river or just to watch the boats go by. As you enter the hotel, an elegantly furnished dining room is to the left and a sophisticated lounge furnished in muted colors to the right. There is a small staircase just off the hallway leading to a few bedrooms, each is spacious and individually decorated with impeccable taste. The rooms in front are more expensive, but also have views of the river: there are three suites which are particularly lovely. Until a century ago, the building used to house a fishermen's guild. Next it was converted to a restaurant and then about 50 years ago it was expanded into a simple hotel. In recent years the hotel was purchased by the very talented Jaegers who totally renovated the entire building; their exquisite taste is responsible for making the hotel so remarkably attractive. Doreen is Chinese and there is a subtle oriental flavor both to the decor and the cuisine. The food is outstanding and attracts many guests from Zurich. The hotel is a member of the very prestigious *Relais & Chateaux* hotel group.

*RHEINHOTEL FISCHERZUNFT*
*Hotelier: Andre & Doreen Jaeger-Soong*
*Rheinquai 8*
*CH-8200 Schaffhausen, Switzerland*
*tel: (053) 25 32 81   fax: (053) 24 32 85*
*11 Rooms: Sfr 150-305*
*Open: All year except end of Jan to mid-Feb*
*Credit Cards: All major*
*On the banks of the Rhine*
*Excellent gourmet restaurant*
*Located 50 km N of Zurich*

Originally a large private residence, the Hotel Margna was built in 1817 by Johann Josty. Johann took advantage of a prime location, building his home on a small spit of land between two lakes. In the summertime there are countless paths along the lake front or leading up to imposing mountain peaks, while in the winter this is a cross-country skier's paradise. Johann Josty's manor is now a beautiful hotel with a gracious touch of sophistication. There are several lounges, a grill restaurant with an open fireplace, plus a second dining room - the Stuva. The hotel has game rooms, a television lounge, and even a whirlpool and steam-bath. Each room is delightful, with warm, cream colored walls, antique accents such as an old sleigh laden with flowers, oriental rugs, a cozy lounge with fireplace and a beautiful dining room with a beamed ceiling. The few guest rooms I saw were charming, with the same ambiance found throughout the hotel. Number 49 has an exceptional view across the meadows and lake. Often I have included hotels knowing that the fussy traveller might not like the rustic nature of my choice. Not so with the Hotel Margna - anyone would love it.

*HOTEL MARGNA*
*Hotelier: Sepp & Dorly Muessgens*
*CH-7515 Sils-Baselgia, Switzerland*
*tel: (082) 4 53 06  fax: (082) 4 54 70*
*72 Rooms: Sfr 200-310*
*Open: Jun to Oct & Dec to Apr*
*Credit Cards: None accepted*
*Lovely old country manor*
*Beautifully situated between 2 lakes*
*Located 200 km E of Zurich*

The ski resort of St Moritz attracts the wealthy, international jet set and is always alive with activity.   The town, in my estimation, is too much of a hodge-podge of styles and tastes jumbled together with new condominiums and nondescript hotels. I have unsuccessfully searched in the past for a wonderful little inn to recommend in St Moritz, so this time I extended my search and was extremely pleased to find a marvelous little inn only a few miles away.   The ardent skier might still want to be right at the tram of St Moritz, but for those who prefer some charm in their accommodations, the answer might well be to overnight at Silvaplana which is only about 6 km to the south.   Mr and Mrs Strahle-Bezzola have recently purchased the inn and have added a restaurant where good meals are served at reasonable rates. They are eager to keep the ambiance of the hotel cozy and to make the mood of the hotel welcoming and warm.   The reception area is small and friendly, with antiques used to accent the decor.   The dining room is especially charming, with dark wooden chairs, yellow tablecloths, and fresh flowers.   The bedrooms are all nice but they vary in style.   My preference is for the rooms, such as number 9 or 10, located in the original part of the hotel, that are richly paneled in wood.

*LA STAILA*
*Hotelier: Familie Strahle-Bezzola*
*CH-7513 Silvaplana*
*Switzerland*
*tel: (082) 48147  fax: (082) 852155-tourist office*
*17 Rooms: Sfr 110-160*
*Open: Jun to Oct & Dec to mid-Apr*
*Credit Cards: MC, VS*
*Close to St Moritz*
*Located 195 km E of Zurich*

Soglio is a picture-perfect village, perched on a narrow mountain ledge over-looking the beautiful Bregaglia Valley. The almost too-perfect image is completed by a church spire stretching into the sky and cows lazily grazing in the mountain meadows. When finally I visited Soglio, I found it in reality even more beautiful than anticipated. The Hotel Palazzo Salis, an imposing box-like mansion, sits smack in the middle of the village in its own square. Although the name implies a "palace", this is really quite a simple hotel, but very nice. The guest rooms are upstairs and only a few in the hotel have a private bath. To accommodate extra guests, various rooms are also scattered throughout the village in annexes. The guest rooms, although simple, are clean and very adequate for an inexpensive hotel. The Palazzo Salis dates back several centuries and maintains the character of yesteryear. A number of hunting trophies proudly decorate the reception area, and a collection of antique spears are artistically arranged on the third floor walls. Settle here and days can be spent following an endless number of paths that explore this gloriously beautiful region. I fell in love with Soglio and consider it one of Switzerland's most picturesque villages and well worth any detour.

*HOTEL PALAZZO SALIS*
*Hotelier: Familie Cadisch*
*CH-7649 Soglio*
*Switzerland*
*tel: (082) 4 12 08*
*15 Rooms: Sfr 108-145 (with 2 meals)*
*Open: May to Oct*
*Credit Cards: None*
*Spectacular mountain village*
*Located 210 km SE of Zurich*

The Hotel Krone, a 13th-century residence, is located in the fascinating, walled medieval town of Solothurn. The building is everything a Swiss inn should be. A cozy exterior with the palest, soft pink facade with contrasting muted green shutters fronted by window boxes overflowing with geraniums sets the quiet mood of the inn. The location too is perfect - facing onto the colorful main square, just opposite Saint Urs Cathedral. The reception area is more formal than the exterior would indicate, but the dining room has a cozy country inn atmosphere and fresh flowers are plentiful in the table settings. Upstairs, a large room is often used for private parties, and there is also a relaxing bar, perfect for a welcome drink. Outside, tables are set in good weather for light meals. The bedrooms are all very similar in decor, with copies of Louis XV furniture that blend nicely with genuine antiques. The more deluxe rooms are especially large and have spacious bathrooms with tubs so big you can almost go swimming - although more expensive, I think they are worth the additional cost.

*HOTEL KRONE*
*Hotelier: Joseph Kung-Roschi*
*Hauptgasse 64*
*CH-4500 Solothurn, Switzerland*
*tel: (065) 22 44 12  fax: (065) 22 37 24*
*42 Rooms: Sfr 130-185*
*Open: All year*
*Credit Cards: All major*
*Hotel Rep: Best Western*
*Rep tel: 800-528-1234*
*Middle of medieval walled city*
*Located 76 km S of Basel*

The town of Verbier, located on a high meadow overlooking the Bagnes Valley, is known to long-distance cross country skiers as the starting point of the "High Road Run", of which Saas-Fee or Zermatt is the terminus. I had always heard that Verbier was a modern town built expressly to satisfy the whims of the ardent skier; therefore, I was pleased and surprised to notice as the car twisted up the road from the valley the many traditional wooden farmhouses that remain and add character to the otherwise modern ski facilities. In the center of town, the Hotel Rosalp is a typical chalet-style hotel. The dining room is beautiful, with wood paneling and tables set with crisp linens and fresh flowers. The overall effect is one of style and chic. All the bedrooms have private baths and are modern in their decor. However, it is the dining that really makes this hotel so very special. The owner, Roland Pierroz, has the reputation of serving some of the very finest food in Switzerland. The Hotel Rosalp is a member of the prestigious *Relais & Chateaux* hotel group.

*HOTEL ROSALP*
*Hotelier: Familie Pierroz*
*CH-1936 Verbier, Switzerland*
*tel: (026) 31 63 23  fax: (026) 31 10 59*
*20 Rooms: Sfr 200-300*
*Open: Jul to Sep & Dec to Apr*
*Credit cards: VS, EC*
*Ski resort, sauna, jacuuzzi, shops*
*Gourmet dining*
*Located 167 km E of Geneva*

If you want to combine resort-style living on the lake and still be within an hour of Lucerne by boat or half an hour by car, then the Park Hotel Vitznau might be your "cup of tea".  It is ideally located in a beautiful park like setting directly on the banks of Lake Lucerne.  This is not a rustic hotel in any way.  Rather, it is sophisticated, with all the amenities that one would expect from a deluxe establishment - a large swimming pool, sauna, tennis courts, garden-golf, and even a children's playground.  The lakeside setting also allows waterskiing, sailing, swimming, and fishing.  The building is like a castle, with turrets, towers, gables, and many nooks and crannies.  A beautiful lawn surrounded by gardens runs down from the hotel to the edge of the lake where a promenade follows the contours of the lake front.  The setting is one of such bliss that it is hard to believe you are so close to the city of Lucerne.  Inside, the lobby, lounge areas, and dining room are beautifully decorated with combinations of wood beams, fireplaces, oriental rugs on gleaming hardwood floors, green plants, and antique accents.

*PARK HOTEL VITZNAU*
*Hotelier: Peter Bally*
*CH-6354 Vitznau, Switzerland*
*tel: (041) 831 322  fax: (041) 831 397*
*98 Rooms: Sfr 370-470*
*Open: mid-Apr to mid-Oct*
*U.S. Rep: Utell International*
*Rep tel: 800-448-8355*
*Elegant Victorian-style hotel*
*Waterfront setting on Lake Lucerne*
*Located 60 km SE of Zurich*

There are no roads into Wengen, so you will be arriving by train.   As you enter the village, you can see the Regina Hotel perched on a knoll above the station.   Since there are no cars in Wengen, a porter from the Regina will bring a cart to take you for the short ride up a winding lane to the hotel.   While I was waiting, I saw one cart pull away brimming with several children, an enormous dog, mother, father and all their luggage.   When you enter the hotel you will probably be reminded of one of the British resorts so popular at the turn of the century.   The downstairs has large, rambling lobbies punctuated with small seating areas with chairs encircling game tables, and a huge fireplace surrounded by overstuffed chairs.   It all looks very "Swiss British".   Our bedroom was quite ordinary EXCEPT FOR THE VIEW.   And what a view.   The "picture" from our balcony was truly one of the most breathtaking I have ever seen: a shelf of velvet green lawn suddenly dropping off to a valley far below.   The opposite side of the valley is walled with granite and laced by waterfalls.   A backdrop of mighty mountains whose peaks are covered in snowy glaciers completes the scene.

The dining room of the Regina is unimaginative and quite modern in decor, lacking any "country inn" atmosphere.   The food was good, but not outstanding...more like plain home cooking.   Why then, you might wonder, with simple food and undistinguished rooms would I include the Regina?   The answer is simple.   I fell in love with the glory of the view, and I fell in love with the owner, Jack Meyer, one of the warmest, old-fashioned hotelier imaginable.   The Regina had been in his family for many generations and for him, running the hotel was far more than a business, it was an art and a way of life.   Contented guests return year after year.   Many coincide their holidays with other guests whom they have met in previous years at the hotel.   Jack ran the hotel more like a house party than a hotel, catering to the special whim of each guest: remembering their favorite room, their favorite bottle of Scotch, their special pillow.   Jack Meyer's father was in the hotel business, as was his grandfather. When I was at the Regina, I asked Mr Meyer if he had sons. "Yes," he said with a disappointed look, "I have two, but neither wanted to follow in the profession. However," he added with a twinkle in his eye, "they both changed their minds and are now in hotel school." Jack Meyer is now retired, but his son Guido Meyer and his wife, Ariane, have bought the hotel and are carrying on with the same famous tradition of genuine hospitality. Guido told me that his father is still frequently at the hotel, continuing to greet his guests and friends of many years.

Guido also says that he is redecorating the rooms, one by one, to a higher standard and very soon all will have been completely redone. Guido also notes that the biggest change in the hotel is in the dinner menu which includes hot and cold starters, salads, soup of the day, a choice of four entrees and dessert buffet.

*HOTEL REGINA*
*Hotelier: Guido Meyer*
*CH-3823 Wengen*
*Switzerland*
*tel: (036) 55 15 12  fax: (036) 755 1574*
*90 Rooms: Sfr 176-240 (with 2 meals)*
*Open: Jun to Oct & Dec to May*
*Credit cards: All major*
*Excellent for Jungfrau excursion*
*Fabulous mountain views*
*Located 143 km S of Zurich*

In the small town of Worb, just a few miles east of Berne, is the Hotel Lowen.   This hotel is positioned at the junction of two busy streets, but, even so, a country charm radiates from its colorful, shuttered exterior.   On the entry level the inn has a number of small, beautiful dining rooms.   Each varies in decor, but all abound with antiques.   Dining is famous in this little inn - attracting dinner guests from all over Switzerland.   (If your base is Berne and Worb proves to be just a day excursion, arrange your trip to include a lunch or dinner stop at the Hotel Lowen).   The accommodations are simple but pleasant.   Antiques adorn the halls and lobbies giving a cheerful, cozy ambiance.   The Hotel Lowen was established over 600 years ago and incredibly has been in the same family for over 11 generations, so it is not surprising that the service and quality of this small inn is so special - a perfect example of one of Switzerland's most highly regarded professions, the hotel business.

*HOTEL LOWEN*
*Hotelier: Familie Bernhard*
*Enggisteinstrasse 3*
*CH-3076 Worb, Switzerland*
*tel: (031) 83 23 03   fax: (031) 83 58 77*
*14 Rooms: Sfr 80-140*
*Closed: 2 weeks in July & 1 week in August*
*U.S. Rep: Romantik Hotels*
*Rep tel: 800-826-0015*
*Renowned for its restaurant*
*Located 105 km W of Zurich*

The Alex Schlosshotel Tenne brims with the charm of a very old, weathered wood facade - accented of course in summer by flowers.   Originally the Tenne appeared in our guide for its excellence of service and fabulous restaurant, in spite of the fact that there were various "jarring" notes such as a gaudy turquoise pool in front and electronic game machines in the lobby.   Therefore I was very pleased to receive a letter from Alex Perren (a former mountain guide who recently purchased the hotel).   He has completely renovated the house from top to bottom except for the dining rooms which have kept their sensational antique ambiance.   The hotel now maintains a more sophisticated decor with the tacky features corrected.   Five new suites have been added - all in alpine style, all with fireplace and balcony.   There are also three new duplex-suites in art nouveau style.   The Tenne is located very close to the train station, and, although there are some lovely views of the mountains, unfortunately, some of the views are marred by the train tracks. Nevertheless, this is one of the most deluxe small hotels in Zermatt and the beautiful ambiance of the restaurant and the excellent facilities make this a recommendation - especially for those of you who enjoy gourmet dining.

*ALEX SCHLOSSHOTEL TENNE*
*Hotelier: Alex Perren*
*CH-3920 Zermatt*
*Switzerland*
*tel: (028) 67 18 01  fax: (028) 67 18 03*
*38 rooms: Sfr 192-440 (with 2 meals)*
*Closed: Oct & May*
*Gourmet restaurant*
*Located 250 km SE of Geneva*

The Hotel Julen is located across the river, an easy walk to the center of Zermatt, but away from the bustle of tourists.  Renovated in 1981, the hotel is owned and operated by Daniela and Paul Julen who have kept the hotel's traditional atmosphere.  It is definitely a wonderful exception to so many of the new hotels which are clean and attractive but do not offer much "olde worlde" charm.  From the moment you enter the lobby and see the cozy fireplace and the comfortable leather sofas, you will feel the mood of relaxation and friendliness.  You will be captivated by the extremely clever use of antiques, flowers and copper pieces.  The bedrooms profit from the use of simple, clean-lined, light wood furniture so typical of traditional Swiss inns and provincial fabrics and puffy comforters create a cozy ambiance.  The rooms in the back are especially desirable.  Although they are more expensive, I suggest asking for one of the balconied rooms on the upper floors with a view of the Matterhorn.  Behind the hotel is a small terrace - an excellent oasis for luxuriating in the sun and mountain air while enjoying the magnificence of the mountains.

*HOTEL JULEN*
*Hotelier: Familie Julen*
*CH-3920 Zermatt, Switzerland*
*tel: (028) 67 24 81  fax: (028) 67 14 81*
*37 Rooms: Sfr 160-240*
*Open: All year*
*Credit cards: All major*
*U.S. Rep: Romantik Hotels*
*Rep tel: 800-826-0015*
*Chalet style - views of the Matterhorn*
*Located 250 km SE of Geneva*

The Seiler family is an integral part of the very heart of Zermatt.  It was back in the mid 1800s when Alexander Seiler ventured into the hotel business with the first hotel in Zermatt - the Monte Rosa.   The following generations have continued in the wonderful tradition of hospitality set by him by expanding the family enterprise to include several of the finest hotels in Zermatt.   Of these, the Hotel Mont Cervin is the most elegant.   As you enter the elaborate front lobby it is hard to believe you could be in a tiny little village: the reception area is decorated with sophisticated charm; the ceilings are high, with lovely paneling in some areas and wooden beams in others; there are flowers everywhere and accents of lovely antiques.   The dining room has a tranquil formality combined with a reputation for excellence of gourmet food and exquisite service.   The hotel has many of the modern amenities such as an indoor swimming pool, a sauna, a solarium, and even a kindergarten in the winter for the supervision of children while their parents enjoy the mountain slopes.

*SEILER HOTEL MONT CERVIN*
*Manager: Urs H. Keller*
*CH-3920 Zermatt*
*Switzerland*
*tel: (028) 66 11 22  fax: (028) 67 28 78*
*132 Rooms: Sfr 250-510 (with 2 meals)*
*Closed: May & Nov*
*Credit cards: All major*
*U.S. Rep: L.H.W.*
*Rep tel: 800-223-6800*
*Indoor pool, sauna*
*Located 250 km SE of Geneva*

The Hotel Monte Rosa is a "must" when discussing the hotels of Zermatt. How could one possibly leave out the original hotel in Zermatt which is so intricately interwoven with the history and romance of this wonderful old village? The Seiler Family owns the hotel, descendants of Alexander Seiler who waved good-bye to the famous Englishman, Edward Whymper, on July 13, 1865 as he began his historic climb to become the first man to conquer the Matterhorn. Back in the 1800s, when Edward Whymper was asked about the best hotel in Zermatt, he always replied, "Go to the Monte Rosa - go to Seiler's". The answer really has not changed much over the past century. The first small hotel owned by Alexander Seiler has now expanded into a tiny family "kingdom" as each generation of Seilers has inherited the genius of hotel management. There are now several Seiler hotels proudly dominating the hotel scene in Zermatt, but it is still the original Monte Rosa which exudes the nostalgia of the old Zermatt - the romantic Zermatt of yore when adventurous young men sought be the first to conquer the mountain giants.

*SEILER HOTEL MONTE ROSA*
*Hotelier: Jurg H Bossart*
*CH-3920 Zermatt, Switzerland*
*tel: (028) 66 11 31  fax: (028) 67 11 60*
*51 Rooms: Sfr 240-390 (with 2 meals)*
*Open: mid-Dec to mid-Apr; mid-Jun to mid-Oct*
*U.S. Rep: Leading Hotels of the World*
*Rep tel: 800-223-6800*
*Zermatt's oldest hotel*
*Located 250 km SE of Geneva*

On my last visit to Zurich I visited the Hotel Chesa Rustica again. I had always admired its location, smack on the banks of the Limmat River, but before I had the impression that the hotel was a bit shabby. However, it seems the hotel has spruced up a bit, and although not luxurious, the hotel has some nice features. An attempt for "olde worlde" atmosphere is felt as one enters the small reception area where an antique trunk cleverly serves as the reception desk. Throughout the hotel, accents of antiques appear such as old clocks, beautiful plate racks, old wooden chests - frequently enhanced by baskets of flowers. The bedrooms are furnished with new wooden furnishings, but with a traditional look. Each bedroom is well-equipped with small refrigerator, direct-dial telephone, radio and TV. There is an especially cozy paneled dining nook where cheese fondue is the specialty, plus a larger more formal restaurant, the Schiff. The windows are supposedly soundproofed, which is a nice addition since the noise of the promenade along the river could be disturbing at night.

*HOTEL CHESA RUSTICA*
*Owner: H. Altorfer-Muller*
*Limmatquai 70*
*CH-8001 Zurich, Switzerland*
*tel: (01) 251 92 91  fax: (01) 261 01 79*
*23 rooms: Sfr 160-230*
*Open: All year*
*Credit cards: All Major*
*U.S. Rep: Romantik Hotels*
*Rep tel: 800-826-0015*
*13th-century building*
*Located in heart of Zurich*

Hotel space in Zurich is sometimes almost impossible to find - so although the Seiler Hotel Neues Schloss (built in 1938) is not an "olde worlde" hotel, it can certainly be recommended as an alternate choice for a place to stay in Zurich. From the outside the hotel is not outstanding - a rather boxy, modern gray building, improved somewhat by flower boxes on the corner windows.  But after spending many hours walking from one end of Zurich to the other looking at dozens of drab, dark hotels, I was immediately captivated by the cheerful elegance of the Neues Schloss with its inviting lobby and lounges decorated with soft pastel carpets, cream colored walls, fresh flowers and traditional furniture accented by a few antiques. The bedrooms too are very pleasant, again with traditional-style furniture.  For dining there is a lovely restaurant, *Le Jardin.*  Another plus: the hotel has a parking garage (there is a charge, but this is a welcome convenience).  The Hotel Neues Schloss is owned by the famous Seiler family who opened the first hotel in Zermatt to serve the mountain climbers.

*SEILER HOTEL NEUES SCHLOSS*
*Hotelier: Bernard Seiler*
*Stockerstrasse 17*
*CH-8022 Zurich, Switzerland*
*tel: (01) 201 65 50  fax: (01) 201 64 18*
*59 Rooms: Sfr 260-300*
*Open: All year*
*Credit cards: All major*
*U.S. Rep: Utell International*
*Rep tel: 800-223-9868*
*New hotel with traditional decor*
*Located near the lake*

The Hotel Tiefenau is a real charmer, an appealing "country inn" away from the bustle of the city yet within easy walking distance to the heart of Zurich's many attractions. Lacy trees frame the yellow facade whose small paned windows are enhanced by dark green shutters. A gay yellow and white striped awning forms a cozy canopy over the front entry. From the moment you enter, you are surrounded by a homey ambiance - nothing slickly commercial, just comfortable chairs, antique chests, oriental rugs, lovely paintings and sunlight streaming in through the many windows. A special surprise is the bedrooms. Each seems so large as to almost be a suite, with plenty of space to relax and read or write letters. There is a small a la carte restaurant "Au Gourmet" serving exceptional food and, when the weather is inviting, meals are served outside in a delightful little garden tucked against the side of the hotel. For guests who want just a snack, pastries, tea, or a light meal, the Cafeteria Hottingen is just a minute's walk from the Tiefenau. A cozy bar serves drinks during the happy hour. Erica and Beat Blumer own and personally manage this exquisite little inn. Their love and attention is evident in every small, perfect detail.

*HOTEL TIEFENAU*
*Hotelier: Erica & Beat Blumer*
*Steinwiesstrasse 8-10*
*CH-8032 Zurich, Switzerland*
*tel: (01) 251 24 09  fax: (01) 251 24 76*
*30 Rooms: Sfr 220-290*
*Open: mid-Jan to mid-Dec*
*Credit cards: All major*
*U.S. Rep: Utell International*
*Rep tel: 800-223-9868*
*Cozy country-style inn*
*Located 5-minute walk to city center*

The Hotel Zum Storchen is so beautifully maintained as a luxury hotel, that at first glance it is difficult to conceive that it has been in operation for over 620 years. Guests enjoy the very most sophisticated luxuries in modern guest rooms, but the hotel still manages to retain a wealth of charm. The Hotel Zum Storchen was strategically built at the narrowest section of the Limmat River as it flowed into Lake Zurich. At this narrow point a bridge was built which became the crossroads of the trade routes to Italy and Germany. Like many of the old inns that revel in tales of history, romance and intrigue, the Zum Storchen is no exception. My favorite story is of Hanns Hennssler, owner of a rival hotel, the Sword Inn: Hanns brought suit against the owner of the Hotel Zum Storchen in 1477 for stealing guests off the streets and enticing them away from his hotel. What a change has taken place over the many centuries - no enticing is needed. Now you are very lucky if the Hotel Zum Storchen can find a room for you.

*HOTEL ZUM STORCHEN*
*Hotelier: J. Philippe Jaussi*
*Am Weinplatz 2*
*CH-8001 Zurich, Switzerland*
*tel: (01) 211 55 10  fax: (01) 211 64 51*
*80 Rooms: Sfr 250-380*
*Open: All year*
*Credit cards: All major*
*U.S. Rep: Utell International*
*Rep tel: 800-448-8355*
*On bank of the Limmat River*
*Located in the center of Zurich*

The Hotel Sonnenberg, located in the hills overlooking Zurich, is a delightful oasis. You can stay at the Sonnenberg for about half the cost of a luxury hotel in Zurich, but the real bonus is the fabulous view overlooking the city and the beautiful lake. Surrounding the hotel are forests, assuring the guest of quiet the whole day.  You can stay at the Sonnenberg just enjoying walks through the woods and the peaceful vistas, but for those who want to sightsee, Zurich is only 15-minutes away by tram. The hotel has many country antiques, giving an appealing welcome from the moment you enter the lobby. The bedrooms are simply decorated without antiques, but quite pleasant.  The dining room in the main hotel is charming, but when the weather is nice, meals are served on the terrace where you can savor the panorama along with an excellent meal.  Besides the dining room in the main building, there is a second dining room in a less attractive modern annex below the hotel.  But, although modern in decor, this dining room has wonderful vistas.  If you don't mind being a short drive from Zurich, the Hotel Sonnenberg is an excellent choice, especially if you are travelling with children, because this is a family-style hotel where children are most welcome and where they can romp in the nearby woodlands.

*HOTEL SONNENBERG*
*Hotelier: Rolf Wismer*
*Aurorastrasse 98*
*CH-8032 Zurich, Switzerland*
*tel: (01) 47 00 47  fax: (01) 262 06 33*
*35 Rooms: Sfr 150-210*
*Open: mid-Jan to mid-Dec*
*Credit cards: All major*
*Panoramic view of Zurich*
*Located on a hillside above Zurich*

# Inn Discoveries from Our Readers

Many hotel recommendations have been sent to us by you, our readers. Some we have included in this edition, others we have not yet had the opportunity to see. We have a rule never to include any hotel, no matter how perfect it sounds, until we have made a personal inspection. This seems a waste of some excellent "tips", so, to solve this dilemma, we are adding to each of our guides a new section of hotels you have seen and loved and have shared with us, but which we have not yet inspected. Thank you for your contributions. Please keep them coming.

| APPENZELL | HOTEL LOWEN | Map: 61 |
| --- | --- | --- |

Hotel Lowen, Familie Sutter, CH-9050 Appenzell, Switzerland; tel: (071) 87 21 87, Sfr 114-146

Appenzell, a small town whose houses are painted with whimsical designs, has always been a favorite town of ours. The area too is gorgeous - brilliant green rolling hills dotted with cows, happily munching the grass while heavy bells strapped round their necks ring with the rhythm of their walk. We are therefore glad to have a reader recommendation to add to our list of hotel possibilities. "In Appenzell we stayed at the Lowen and it was perfectly charming with all the new bauermalerei furniture in the rooms." *Recommended by Joan Brooks, Germany.*

Arvenhotel Waldeck, Familie Glaus-Casty, CH-7018 Flims-Waldhaus, Switzerland; tel: (081) 39 12 28; 29 rooms; Sfr 136-160

The Arvenhotel Waldeck in Flims-Waldhaus is highly recommended as a small inn - simple but filled with warmth and "olde worlde" charm.   Many antiques are used throughout and the owner makes his guests "feel like his friends".   The inn was completely renovated inside a few years ago, but graciously maintains the charming country inn ambiance.   The owner is also the chef and the food is exceptional. *Recommended by Elsy Manciak.*

Engiadina, Egon Sulger, CH-7551 Ftan, Switzerland; tel: (084) 9 04 34; Sfr 160-200 (price includes 2 meals)

"We had the very good fortune to have an unplanned but delightful stay at the Hotel Engiadina in Ftan.   Ftan (which we heard pronounced about ten different ways) is on the high road between Guarda and Bad Scoul.   It was recommended by the innkeeper at the Piz Buin Hotel in Guarda as having an excellent kitchen.   We not only had wonderful meals during our stay, but lodged in a nice room, number 15, with a beautiful south and east facing view from our room and balcony.   For our two night stay, we were able to be on their half pension (2 meals) arrangement which made our room and dining cost less than $100 a night." *Recommended by Frank and Linda Brennan.*

Hotel Haus Paradies, Brigitte & Roland Johri, CH-7551 Ftan, Switzerland; tel: (084) 9 13 25   fax: (084) 9 17 74; 13 rooms, 8 apartments; Sfr 280-320

The Hotel Haus Paradies is superbly positioned on a plateau overlooking the beautiful Engandine Valley, in the far eastern corner of Switzerland - almost to the Austrian border. This hotel is deluxe incorporating modern furnishings (especially in the bedrooms) with an "olde worlde" ambiance created through the use of accent antiques, beamed ceilings and beautiful arrays of flowers. The bedrooms are starkly modern - but not the views, which are just spectacular. The proprietor, Roland Johri, is a renowned chef and the food is truly a gourmet's delight. *Recommended by Mme G Pierre.*

Gletschergarten, Familie Breitenstein, CH-3818, Grindelwald, Switzerland; tel: (036) 53 17 21;   28 rooms;   Sfr 145-185

"As a constant traveller and devotee of your books I want to share a discovery with you.   During a trip through Switzerland we drove to Grindelwald.   To our delight, the 90-year-old Gletschergarten was just opening for the summer and accepted us for the night. The inn is so warm, clean and attractive. Our hosts, the Breitensteins, the third generation owners, were so welcoming and relaxed, despite a thousand duties in opening their huge chalet, that I wanted to urge you to include their hotel in your next Swiss edition."   Note: from the brochure the hotel looks charming - we'll be eager to check it out on our next trip to Switzerland. *Recommended by AE (Reader requested we only use her initials)*

Hotel Krebs, Familie Krebs, Bahnhofstrasse 4, CH-3800 Interlaken, Switzerland, tel: (036) 22 71 61, fax: (036) 23 24 65, 51 rooms, Sfr 164-184

"Switzerland is our favorite destination.  About 12 years ago we found "our hotel", the Hotel Krebs in Interlaken.  Because it is on the main street, the front rooms can be a little noisy, but you can see the Jungfrau, Eiger and Monk (mountains) from the front rooms, so it depends on what is important to you.  Our favorite is number 4, a corner front room with twin beds, large closet, small table, a couch and chest of drawers.  The hotel, in operation about 150 years, has creaky floors, lovely old family antiques, handmade inlaid tables and lovely bouquets of flowers throughout.  The dining room is superb.  We have tried all of the hotels and restaurants in Interlaken and always come back to the Krebs for the best food and service." *Recommended by Margie Simmons.*

Hotel Baren, Fritz Zurschmiede, Interlaken-Wilderswil, CH-3812, Switzerland, tel: (036) 22 35 21, fax: (036) 22 35 44,  50 rooms, Sfr 104-135

"Just outside the bustling town of Interlaken is the friendly Hotel Baren which has been in the Zurschmiede family for five generations - dating back to the time when it catered to guests arriving by horse and carriage.  Today Fritz Zurschmiede, the charming host, points out the original license and old family photos as he leads guests up the wide wooden stairway to the airy, spacious rooms.  This is a wonderfully atmospheric and welcoming base from which to explore the Interlaken and Grindelwald areas." *Recommended by Kirsten Price*

| KLOSTERS | HOTEL WALSERHOF | Map: 56 |
|---|---|---|

Hotel Walserhof, Beat & Gabi Bolliger, CH-7250 Klosters, Switzerland,
tel: (083) 44242; fax: (083) 41437; 11 rooms plus 1 suite; Sfr 150-180

"The Hotel Walserhof, although newly constructed, is built in traditional Grison country style. This charming inn provides all the advantages of the very latest comfort. The hotel has achieved much acclaim for its outstanding kitchen and has been featured in many gourmet magazines. Beat Bolliger, the owner, is the chef and he is a member of the Chaine de Rotisseurs and the Academie Suisse des Gastronoms. The decor is outstanding with decorator-perfect color coordinated country antiques in the cozy beamed-ceilinged dining rooms." *Recommended by Carol Trefethen.*

| LAAX | SPORTHOTEL LARISCH | Map: 60 |
|---|---|---|

Sporthotel Larisch, Herfried Kern, CH-7031 Laax, Switzerland,
tel: (086) 3 47 47; fax: (086) 3 41 13; 32 rooms; Sfr 160

"The Sporthotel Larisch is another mountain lovers' hideaway. This small chalet-style hotel is recommended as "an especially sweet" inn filled with warmth and charm. The owner is also the manager and takes excellent care of his guests and is described as "wonderfully friendly and helpful and the food superior". *Recommended by Elsy Manciak.*

Hotel Rebstock, Sankt-Leodegar-Platz, CH-6000 Lucerne, Switzerland, tel: (041) 51 35 81, fax: (041) 51 39 17, 28 rooms, Sfr 200

"I stopped in to the Hotel Zum Rebstock and asked to see a room. The rooms I was shown were quite small, very clean, modern and, generally speaking, nondescript. I wasn't overly impressed, but I made a reservation as I knew I would be returning to Lucerne with my husband the following week. When we actually checked into the hotel a week later, we had a most pleasant surprise. We were taken back to our room (which I believe was number 61) through a small, out-of-the-way sitting area and back to a tucked-away corner of the hotel. In this section there were several rooms with heavy wooden doors that my 6'4" husband had to stoop down considerably to go through. Our room was totally unlike the others I had previously been shown. It had a lovely antique armoire, a small separate sitting area located in a turret and a wood-beamed ceiling that gave the room an almost Hansel and Gretel quality." *Recommended by Shelly Lewis.*

Hotel Balances & Bellevue, Weinmarkt, CH-6000 Lucerne, Switzerland, tel: (041) 51 18 51; 70 rooms; Sfr 200-260

The Balances & Bellevue is located directly on the banks of the River Reuss, smack in the middle of Lucerne. Many times we have admired its superb location and tremendously intriguing fancy facade. However, last time we made an inspection, the guest rooms were a bit shabby. Recently we have received several letters from readers saying the hotel has been refurbished and is now quite nice. *The editor*

## MURREN       ALPINA HOTEL                          Map: 31

Alpina Hotel, Familie Taugwalder-Meier, CH-3825 Murren, Switzerland; tel: (036) 55 13 61; Sfr 156-187 (price includes 2 meals)

"A favorite town of ours in the Jungfrau region is Murren, right across the valley from the town of Wengen, where there is a very nice hotel, the Alpina." Editor's note: We are very eager to check out the Alpina. Although the hotel looks quite ordinary in decor and of recent vintage, the view from the balconied bedrooms and from the dining room looks positively breathtaking. The hotel appears to cling to the side of the mountain with an unobstructed vista. *Recommended by Deirdre Colby.*


## MURTEN       HOTEL WEISSES KREUZ                    Map: 9

Hotel Weisses Kreuz, Daniel Bischoff, Rathaugasse 31, CH-3280 Murten, Switzerland, tel: (037) 71 26 41   fax: (037) 71 28 66; 27 rooms; Sfr 130-150

"In Murten we stayed at the Weisses Kreuz because we wanted to be in town. It was a comfortable hotel just above the boat dock." Editor's note: We love the quaint medieval walled village of Murten and it is nice to have another suggestion for a hotel. The brochure portrays a very attractive small hotel with a liberal use of antiques, oriental carpets, dining terrace and spacious rooms with large windows and a splendid view to the lake. (We feature in our guide the Le Vieux Manoir au Lac which is located just outside Murten. Some prefer to be closer to the action.) *Recommended by Donald and Carolyn Beimdiek.*

Hotel Munsterhof, Familie Meyer, CH-7537 Mustair, Switzerland;
tel: (082) 85 541; 19 rooms; Sfr 70-110

The Hotel Munsterhof is located directly across the street from the Hotel Chasa Chalavaina (which is featured in our guide). The Hotel Munsterhof, a 100-year-old inn, is furnished in traditional-style furniture including many antiques. The country-style decor creates a cozy ambiance. In some of the bedrooms there are very attractive wooden beds and painted Armories. The family is totally involved in the operation and the preparation of the meals, with their specialties being cuisine from the Grison region. The owners speak English and pride themselves on good service. *Recommended by Jon Fasser.*

Hotel Kreuz, CH-3713 Reichenbach, Switzerland, tel: (033) 76 11 06; Sfr 90

"We are thrilled to say that the Hotel Kreuz surpassed our wildest expectations. With a bath, the double costs Sfr 87. What was the special surprise was the outstandingly excellent meal. I have worked in the restaurant industry in New York City for 30 years and have dined at all of the best, including 5-star restaurants. I cannot think of any place before that could begin to compete with the excellent meal at the Hotel Kreuz." Editor's note: The brochure shows a very simple, rather modern facade, but such a glowing recommendation certainly warranted its inclusion. *Recommended by Roberta Lee.*

Villetta Capolina, Familie Schweizer, CH-7536 Santa Maria, Switzerland,
tel (c/o Hotel Chasa Capol) tel: (082) 8 57 28; 8 rooms; Sfr 110

The Villetta Capolina has been highly recommended as a small pension recently
opened across the street from the Hotel Chasa Capol.  This sounds like a real
winner for travellers who want a budget hotel with style.  None of the bedrooms
has a private bath, but we are advised they are pleasantly furnished with a country
style.  Two of the bedrooms are especially romantic in decor.  There is also an
apartment with kitchenette for those who would like to do a little cooking.  This
might be a good choice for families.  We welcome more feedback.  *Recommended
by Alice Wilkinson.*

Hotel Park Villa, Max Schlumpf, Parkstrasse 18, CH-8200 Schaffhausen,
Switzerland; tel: (053) 25 27 37; fax: (053) 24 12 53; 21 rooms; Sfr 128-190

"In Schaffhausen we stayed at the Park Villa.  We were made to feel like one of the
family."  Editor's note:  The Park Villa hotel does look exceptionally nice.  It
used to be a private mansion until converted into a hotel about 20 years ago.  The
hotel has recently changed management and now Max Schlumpf has renovated all
of the rooms.  One floor has antique furniture, others are in modern Italian style.
The restaurant and bar are furnished with antiques.  According to the hotel, "We
manage the hotel in a family and friendly way to give our guests a welcome and
happy feeling to be staying here and enjoy looking after them personally."
*Recommended by Donald and Carolyn Beimdiek.*

La Soglina, CH-7610 Soglio, Switzerland; tel: (082) 4 16 08; 31 rooms; Sfr 80-104

The town of Soglio is "postcard-perfect". Snuggled on a plateau high above the valley, this cluster of medieval homes and charming little church create one of the prettiest scenes in Switzerland. We have one hotel already recommended in Soglio (the Palazzo Salis), but frequently space is limited and reservations not available. Therefore, we are pleased to include an alternate choice to this gem of a town. Owned by the Nass-Schumacher family are three choices of accommodations: Casa Soglina, Pension Soglina, and Stua Granda. Although they are not built within one of Soglio's characterful old buildings (as is the Palazzo Salis), they are highly recommended by several readers. The freshly scrubbed guest rooms are pleasant with fluffy comforters on the beds. The food is very good and there is a lovely dining terrace. *Recommended by Dr and Mrs Shipley*

STEIN AM RHEIN-HEMISHOFEN    LANDGASTHOF BACCHUS  Map: 62

Landgasthof Bacchus, Kurt Specht, CH-8261 Stein am Rhein-Hemishofen, Switzerland; tel: (054) 41 24 05; fax: (021) 921 75 08; 5 rooms; Sfr 80-90

One of the most appealing villages in Switzerland is the walled village, Stein am Rhein, located on the banks of the Rhein. The main square is surrounded by elaborately painted medieval buildings. Unfortunately, there is a very limited selection of places to spend the night. Therefore we were happy to hear of the Landgasthof Bacchus. Although not in the center of the village, this very old inn is located only a short taxi-ride (or 30-minute walk) away. The inn sits on the rise of a hill above the Rhein. The stuccoed exterior is handsomely accented with exposed wooden beams providing a rustic ambiance appropriate to the inn's earlier function as a barn. The interior has been completely refurbished and each of the modernly furnished bedrooms has a private bath. The owner, Kurt Specht, is extremely gracious and speaks excellent English. Note: we are looking forward to seeing this hotel on our next trip to Switzerland and, in the meantime, would greatly appreciate readers' comments. *The editor*

## VEVEY          HOTEL DU LAC                                    Map: 6

Hotel du Lac, P. Ehrensperger, Rue d'Italie, CH-1800 Vevey, Switzerland; tel: (021) 51 10 41, fax: (021) 921 75 08; 53 rooms; Sfr 175-265

When speaking to Swiss friends, they said that we must not leave out the Hotel Du Lac, a favorite of theirs and one of the most historic hotels along the lake. Since it first opened its doors in 1868, the Hotel du Lac has been an integral part of the resort community of Vevey, hosting many of the world's celebrities including, Henryk Sienkewiez, author of *Quo Vadis*, who lived here from 1914 to 1916. The public rooms of the Hotel du Lac are formal with high ceilings and sedate furniture. The guest rooms have lovely views of Lake Geneva.

# Index - Alphabetically by Hotel

*Index Alphabetically by Hotel*

| HOTEL | TOWN | Page |
|---|---|---|
| PARK VILLA, HOTEL | Schaffhausen | 235 |
| POST HOTEL ROSSLI | Gstaad | 74, 173 |
| REBSTOCK, HOTEL | Lucerne | 232 |
| REGINA, HOTEL | Wengen | 71, 215-216 |
| RHEINHOTEL FISCHERZUNFT | Schaffhausen | 91, 130, 208 |
| ROSALP, HOTEL | Verbier | 77, 213 |
| ROTE ROSE | Regensberg | 89, 200-201 |
| ROYAL HOTEL BELLEVUE | Kandersteg | 72, 181 |
| SANTIS, HOTEL | Appenzell | 133, 149 |
| SCHUSSEL, HOTEL | Lucerne | 190 |
| SEILER HOTEL MONT CERVIN | Zermatt | 142, 220 |
| SEILER HOTEL MONTE ROSA | Zermatt | 78, 221 |
| SEILER HOTEL NEUES SCHLOSS | Zurich | 223 |
| SONNENBERG, HOTEL | Zurich-Sonnenberg | 226 |
| SPORTHOTEL LARISCH | Laax | 231 |
| STAR and POST HOTEL | Amsteg | 148 |
| STERN, HOTEL | Chur | 158-159 |
| TAMARO, HOTEL | Ascona | 151 |
| TIEFENAU, HOTEL | Zurich | 135, 224 |
| VICTORIA, HOTEL | Glion | 124, 166 |
| VICTORIA JUNGFRAU, HOTEL | Interlaken | 180 |
| VILLA MARGHERITA | Lugano-Bosco | 193 |
| VILLA PRINCIPE LEOPOLDO | Lugano | 192 |
| VILLETTA CAPOLINA | Santa Maria | 235 |
| WALDHAUS, HOTEL | Horw-Oberruti | 178 |
| WALDHOTEL FLETSCHHORN | Saas-Fee | 110, 202-203 |
| WALSERHOF, HOTEL | Klosters | 231 |
| WEISSES KREUZ, HOTEL | Murten | 233 |
| WILDEN MANN HOTEL | Lucerne | 52, 137, 188-189 |
| ZUM STORCHEN, HOTEL | Zurich | 50, 225 |
| ZUM WILDEN MANN, HOTEL | Baden | 153 |

# Index - Alphabetically by Town

| TOWN | HOTEL | Page |
|------|-------|------|
| GSTAAD | Post Hotel Rossli | 74, 173 |
| GSTAAD-SCHONRIED | Hotel Alpenrose | 174 |
| GSTAAD-SCHONRIED | Hotel Ermitage Golf Solbad | 175 |
| GSTEIG-GSTAAD | Hotel Baren | 106, 176 |
| GUARDA | Hotel Meisser | 118, 177 |
| HORW-OBERRUTI | Hotel Waldhaus | 178 |
| INTERLAKEN | Hotel Baren | 230 |
| INTERLAKEN | Hotel du Lac | 138, 179 |
| INTERLAKEN | Hotel Krebs | 230 |
| INTERLAKEN | Hotel Victoria Jungfrau | 180 |
| KANDERSTEG | Royal Hotel Bellevue | 72, 181 |
| KLEINE SCHEIDEGG | Kleine Scheidegg Hotel | 182 |
| KLOSTERS | Hotel Chesa Grishuna | 83, 183 |
| KLOSTERS | Hotel Walserhof | 231 |
| KUSSNACHT am Rigi | Hotel du Lac Seehof | 104, 184 |
| LAAX | Sporthotel Larisch | 231 |
| LANGNAU im EMMENTAL | Hotel Hirschen | 185 |
| LENZERHEIDE | Hotel Guarda Val | 186 |
| LUCERNE | Hotel Balances & Bellevue | 232 |
| LUCERNE | Hotel Chateau Gutsch | 69, 187 |
| LUCERNE | Hotel Rebstock | 232 |
| LUCERNE | Hotel Schussel | 190 |
| LUCERNE | Wilden Mann Hotel | 52, 137, 188-189 |
| LUGANO | Hotel Albergo Ticino | 63, 144, 191 |
| LUGANO | Villa Principe Leopoldo | 192 |
| LUGANO-BOSCO | Villa Margherita | 193 |
| LUGANO-CASTAGNOLA | Elvezia al Lago | 113, 194 |
| LUGANO-MORCOTE | Hotel Carina | 195-196 |
| MURREN | Alpina Hotel | 233 |
| MURTEN | Hotel Weisses Kreuz | 233 |
| MURTEN | Le Vieux Manoir au Lac | 96, 126, 197 |
| MUSTAIR | Hotel Chasa Chalavaina | 198 |

*Index Alphabetically by Town*

*Index Alphabetically by Town*

# INN DISCOVERIES FROM OUR READERS

Future editions of *KAREN BROWN'S COUNTRY INN GUIDES* are going to continue to include a list of hotels recommended by you, our readers. We receive many letters describing wonderful inns you have discovered; however, we never feature any hotel as one of our own recommendations until we have had the opportunity to make a personal inspection. This seems a waste of some marvelous "tips". Therefore, in order to give you as much valuable information as possible, we now have a section called "Inn Discoveries from Our Readers". If you have a favorite discovery you would be willing to share with other travellers who love to travel the "inn way", please let us hear from you and include the following:

1. *Your name, address and telephone number.*

2. *Name, address and telephone number of "your inn".*

3. *Brochure or picture of inn (we cannot return material).*

4. *Written permission to use an edited version of your description.*

5. *Would you want your name, city and state included in the book?*

We are constantly updating and revising all of our guide books. We would appreciate comments on any of your favorites. The types of inns we would love to hear about are those with special old-world ambiance, charm and atmosphere. We need a brochure or picture so that we can select those which most closely follow the mood of our guides. We look forward to hearing from you. Thank you.

Karen Brown's Country Inn Guides, Post Office Box 70, San Mateo, CA 94401
Tel: (415) 342-9117    Fax: (415) 342-9153

# Karen Brown's Country Inn Guides

## The Most Reliable & Informative Series on Country Inns

Detailed itineraries guide you through the countryside and suggest a cozy inn for each night's stay. In the hotel section, every listing has been inspected and chosen for its romantic ambiance. Charming accommodations reflect every price range, from budget hideaways to deluxe palaces.

# *Order Form*

## KAREN BROWN'S COUNTRY INN GUIDES

Please ask in your local bookstore for KAREN BROWN'S COUNTRY INN guides.
If the books you want are unavailable, you may order directly from the publisher.

*AUSTRIAN COUNTRY INNS & CASTLES  $12.95*

*CALIFORNIA COUNTRY INNS & ITINERARIES  $12.95*

*ENGLISH, WELSH & SCOTTISH COUNTRY INNS  $12.95*

*EUROPEAN COUNTRY CUISINE - ROMANTIC INNS & RECIPES  $10.95*

*EUROPEAN COUNTRY INNS - BEST ON A BUDGET  $14.95*

*FRENCH COUNTRY BED & BREAKFASTS  $12.95*

*FRENCH COUNTRY INNS & CHATEAUX  $12.95*

*GERMAN COUNTRY INNS & CASTLES  $12.95*

*IRISH COUNTRY INNS  $12.95*

*ITALIAN COUNTRY INNS & VILLAS  $12.95*

*PORTUGUESE COUNTRY INNS & POUSADAS  $12.95*

*SCANDINAVIAN COUNTRY INNS & MANORS  $12.95*

*SPANISH COUNTRY INNS & PARADORS  $12.95*

*SWISS COUNTRY INNS & CHALETS  $12.95*

*Name* _____   *Street* _____

*City* _____   *State* _____  *Zip* _____

*Add $2.00 for the first book and .50 for each additional book for postage & packing.*
*California residents add 6 1/2% sales tax.*
*Indicate the number of copies of each title.  Send in form with your check to:*

KAREN BROWN'S COUNTRY INN GUIDES
P.O Box 70
San Mateo, CA 94401
Tel: (415) 342-9117      Fax: (415) 342-9153

*This guide is especially written for the individual traveller who wants to plan his own vacation. However, should you prefer to join a group, Town and Country - Hillsdale Travel can recommend tours using country inns with romantic ambiance for many of the nights' accommodation. Or, should you want to organize your own group (art class, gourmet society, bridge club, church group, etc.) and travel with friends, custom tours can be arranged using small hotels with special charm and appeal. For further information please call:*

*Town & Country - Hillsdale Travel*
*16 East Third Avenue*
*San Mateo, California 94401*

*(415) 342-5591*
*Outside California 800-227-6733*

# BACKGROUND OF A SMALL PUBLISHING COMPANY

Many readers ask about the background of Karen Brown's Country Inn guides. It all began fourteen years ago. With a love of travel and a desire to perfect her French, Karen said farewell to her room mates at college, packed her bags, and headed for Europe. France became "home" for nine months as she roamed thousands of miles in her little blue Fiat ferreting out the most appealing places to stay - charming little inns and romantic chateaux. Each night, tucked in bed, Karen would pull out pen and notebook to record her day's adventures. Upon returning to California, Karen polished her guide, then enlisted the help of a college friend to sketch each inn and another to teach her design and paste-up skills. Next came a trip to the bank. With a staged courage, backed up with a projection of sales, Karen convinced a local bank that her book would sell 2,000 copies, enough to pay off the necessary loan to cover publication costs. *French Country Inns & Chateaux* went to press. The loan was quickly paid off and Karen's career was launched.

*French Country Inns & Chateaux* was an immediate success. It was the first book on the market dedicated to guiding the discerning reader to the most romantic hideaways in France. Next came a book on Britain, then Switzerland, Italy, Austria, Germany, Spain, Portugal, Ireland and Scandinavia. As Travel Press grew and the list of titles expanded, more help was needed. Karen first solicited the aid of her mother, Clare Brown, a travel agent whose expertise was planning European vacations. Next to join the tiny staff was June Brown who, although not related to Karen, is a devoted friend whose marvelous English wit transforms the dullest of duties into merry tasks. Another friend of Karen's, the very talented, Australian-born Barbara Tapp, adds greatly to the series with her wonderful art work. For many years, to keep costs at a minimum, the publishing company worked out of the family garage: paste up was on the ping pong table; maps covered the walls; the dog stretched out asleep beneath the desk.

Travel Press no longer operates out of the garage. It has moved to much fancier surroundings: upstairs to a large room which used to be the bedroom for Karen's three brothers. Files fill niches where beds once resided. A "hand-made" light table donated by a friend dominates one corner. Three computers click away turning out camera ready text. When not travelling, the "Three Musketeers" of the publishing staff keep busy every moment of the day and often into the wee hours of the morning. Work is shared equally: preliminary research, travel to Europe to inspect hotels, writing, editing, computer input, printing, paste-up, promotions, bookkeeping, sales and distribution. The German shepherd, Fritz, has also moved upstairs and plops on the floor with only an occasional stretch then nudge at the elbow for a bit of a attention.

The staff has continued to grow. The newest members are not the most conducive to work patterns. Karen is now married and has two little ones: Alexandra, a toddler of two and Richard, a most active lad who will soon be a year old. June too has a new baby, little Clare, who blissfully sleeps away in her bassinet, lulled to sleep by the rhythm of the humming computers. Somehow the work is still churned out and every critical path is right on target. Deadlines are miraculously always met.

Although tiny, and still very *homespun* in its setting, Travel Press is professional and unique. There are very few publishers of guide books that control their publications from research to the final paste up. Because all of the work is done "in house" the books are never stale - they are always in print in the year they are researched. Another bonus is the complete control. Changes can be made instantly and revisions can entered within minutes before the text goes to press.

From this simple little enterprise emerges the finest guide books to Europe for the discriminating traveller looking for romantic places to stay and suggestions for superb countryside itineraries. Now Travel Press has "come home" with the publication of *California Country Inns & Itineraries* which has proved to be an instant success. But Karen's first release, *French Country Inns & Chateaux*, continues to be the best seller of all. And Karen's books (also published in London) are seen in bookstores throughout the world.

Karen Brown (Herbert) was born in Denver, but has spent most of her life in the San Francisco Bay area where she now lives with her husband, Rick, their little girl, Alexandra, and baby son, Richard. Taking a year off from college, Karen travelled to Europe and wrote French Country Inns & Chateaux, the first in what has grown to be an extremely successful series of 14 guide books on charming places to stay. For many years Karen has been planning to open her own country inn. Her dream will soon come to reality - Karen and her husband, Rick, have bought a beautiful piece of property on the coast south of San Francisco and are working with an architect to design the "perfect" little inn which will be furnished with the antiques she has been collecting for many years and will incorporate her wealth of information on just what makes an inn very special. Karen and Rick are looking forward to welcoming guests and friends to their inn.